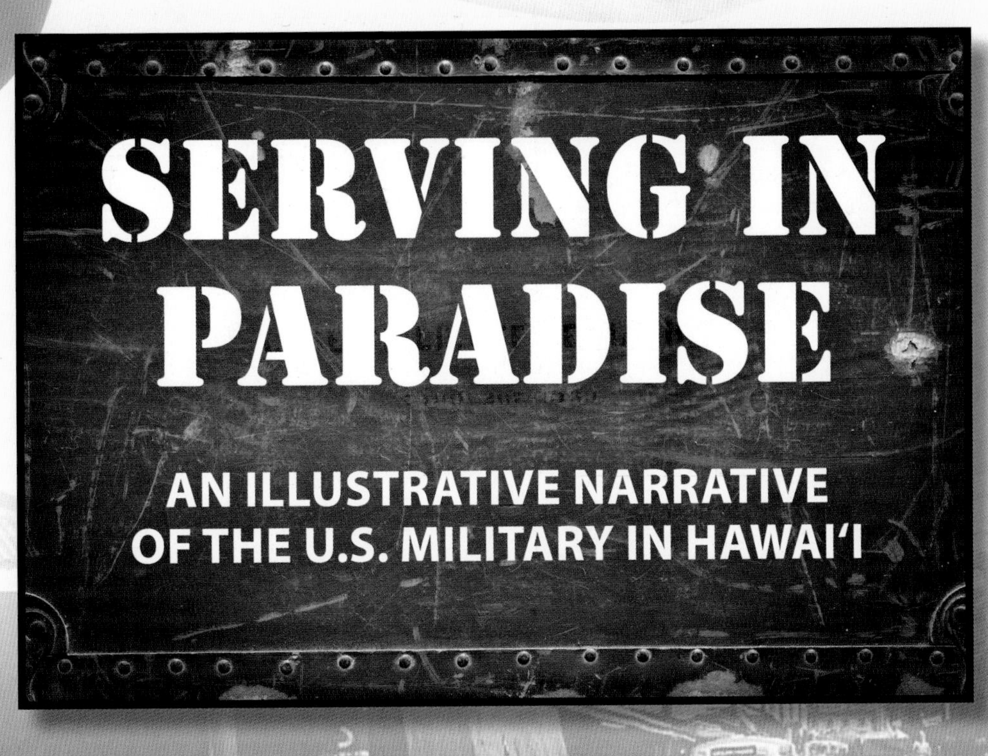
SERVING IN
PARADISE
AN ILLUSTRATIVE NARRATIVE
OF THE U.S. MILITARY IN HAWAI'I

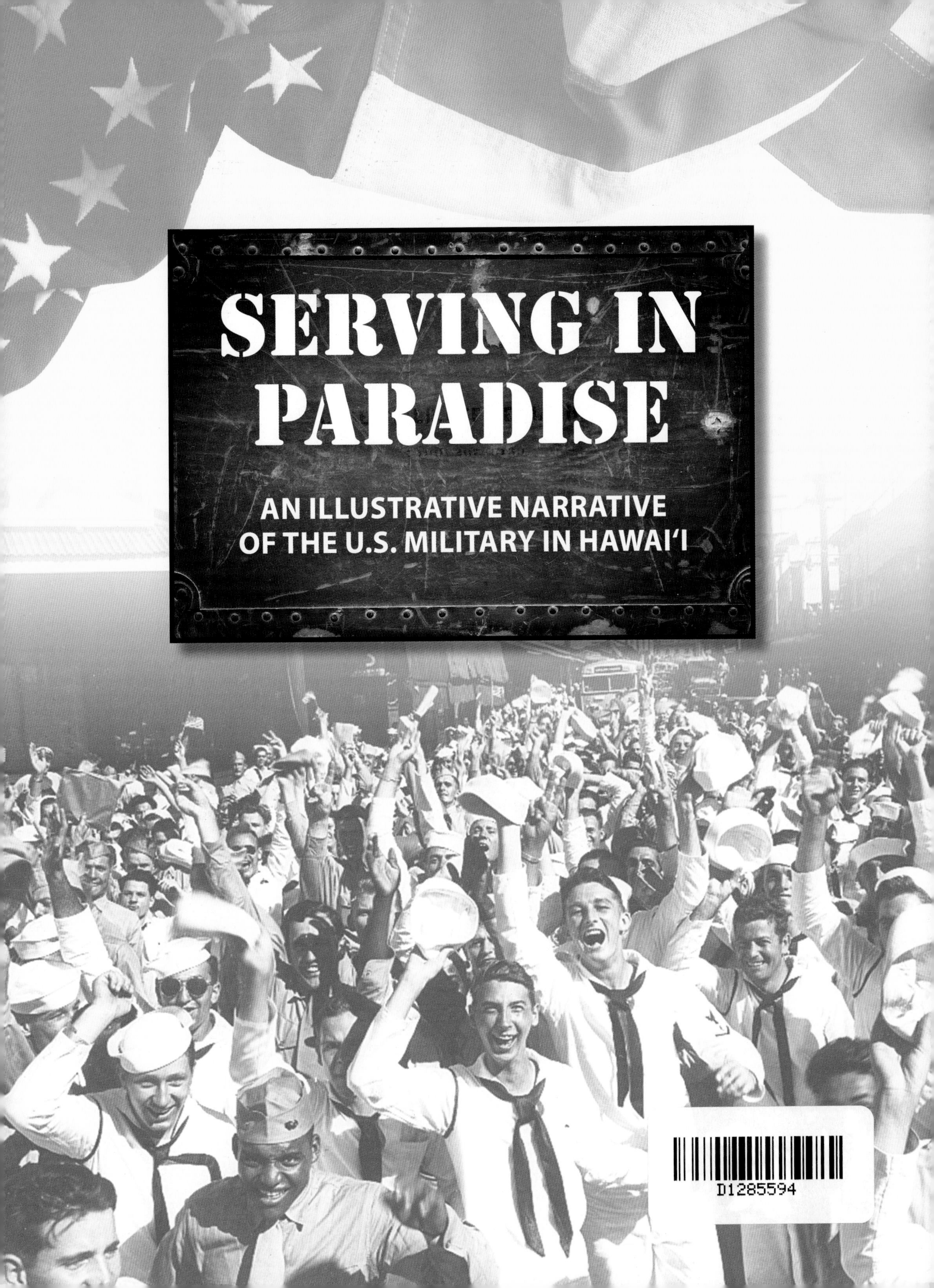

On V-J Day, August 14, 1945, word came at 1:42 p.m. that Allied Forces were "victorious in the air, on the land and over the seas." Civilians and military personnel alike received the news of Japan's surrender with wild jubliation. Within minutes, over 50,000 phone calls were made on O'ahu as friends and family spread the news. [National Archives]

AN ILLUSTRATIVE NARRATIVE OF THE U.S. MILITARY IN HAWAI'I

CHRIS COOK

with a Foreword by
LtGen Emerson Gardner USMC Ret.

Mutual Publishing

ISBN-13: 978-1939487-01-8
Library of Congress Control Number: 2016906227

Design by Jane Gillespie

First Printing, September 2016

Mutual Publishing, LLC
1215 Center Street, Suite 210
Honolulu, Hawai'i 96816
Ph: (808) 732-1709
Fax: (808) 734-4094
e-mail: info@mutualpublishing.com
www.mutualpublishing.com

Printed in South Korea

**To all the
men and women
who have served,
especially those who
made the ultimate
sacrifice.**

TABLE OF CONTENTS

Prologue

Territorial Days

The Pearl Harbor Atttack

Hawai'i at War

Post War Hawai'i

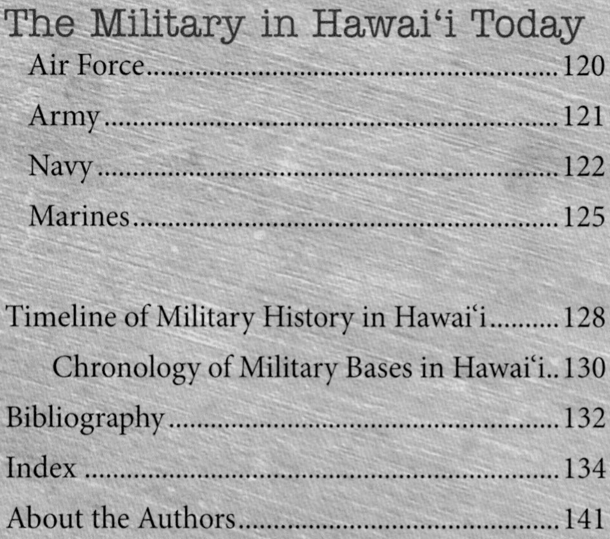

The Military in Hawai'i Today

FOREWORD

Over 120 years before December 7, 1941, U.S. Navy ships began visiting Hawaiʻi, following American whaling ships and early Pacific trade. American navy ships were neither the first military ships nor even the most frequent to visit the islands in the early 19th century as all the major European powers sought to gain control of the strategically located islands. Over the years, however, American geographic proximity and cultural influence pushed aside competitors for dominance within the Hawaiian kingdom.

LtGen Emerson Gardner USMC Ret. (center) meeting with the Adjutant General of the Hawaiʻi National Guard (right) and the Honolulu FBI Special Agent in Charge (left). During his tour as Director for Operations at U.S. Pacific Command at Camp Smith, Gen Gardner coordinated joint military and interagency operations in the Pacific theater. [LtGen Emerson Gardner USMC Ret.]

A significant change in the nature of the U.S. military presence in Hawaiʻi came in 1898 with the temporary stationing of American troops as part of the far-flung, but one-sided, Spanish-American War. Formal annexation came later that same year. Since then, the history of the U.S. military and Hawaiʻi have become even more interwoven as the islands have evolved from a remote Pacific outpost to an integral part of the United States itself.

Serving in Paradise: An Illustrative Narrative of the U.S. Military in Hawaiʻi depicts Hawaiʻi's transformation in strategic importance through the lens of the history of the U.S. military in the islands—from its first permanent bases in the early 20th century to its role as focal point for U.S. strategic interests in the 21st century. The book also covers in detail the war memorials and military museums that provide the evidence of the historical development of the military in the state. No stay in Hawaiʻi is complete without a visit to Ford Island for a tour of the USS *Arizona,* the USS *Missouri,* the USS *Bowfin,* and the Pacific Aviation Museum or to Punchbowl National Cemetery, the final resting place of so many of our war heroes.

There is, however, much more to the military story in Hawaiʻi than just the historical events that have taken place here. The U.S. Pacific Command located at Camp Smith is the fulcrum on which President Obama has rebalanced the national strategy towards the Asia Pacific. The Air Force's most capable fighter, the F-22, is home-based at Hickam Air Force Base. The Marine Corps is basing its most capable helicopter, the MV-22 tiltrotor, at Kāneʻohe Bay, and by 2019, 60 percent of the U.S. Navy will be based in the Pacific and commanded from Pacific Fleet Headquarters at Pearl Harbor.

As a senior Marine officer, I know that the military story cannot be told without talking about people. Today, Hawaiʻi is home to over 50,000 active duty military personnel and over 18,000 Department of Defense civilian employees. Over 200,000 family members ("dependents") live with them in housing on 11 military bases as well as within the civilian community. More than 20 percent of the 1.43 million residents of Hawaiʻi are currently a part of, or are connected, to the U.S. military. Alongside those nearly 300,000 persons currently connected to the military are another 110,000 veterans who have served in the past and now live in Hawaiʻi.

The pages and photos of *Serving in Paradise* illuminate an important aspect of American and Hawaiian history and show the mutual importance of the U.S. military to Hawaiʻi and of Hawaiʻi to the U.S. military.

—LtGen Emerson Gardner USMC Ret.

INTRODUCTION

The military heritage of Hawai'i spans a millennium, from the legendary days of ancient Hawaiian kings to the high-tech warriors of the twenty-first century. The men and women of Hawai'i, and those from elsewhere who have served in the Islands, have shown courage, bravery, dedication, sacrifice, and great skill in defending both the Hawaiian Islands and the United States. *Serving in Paradise: An Illustrative History of the U.S. Military in Hawai'i* tells their story in words and select historic photos and illustrations, as well as guiding you to the memorials, monuments, and museums that honor and portray this heritage.

The Prisoners of War and Missing in Action Recognition Day Ceremony at the National Memorial Cemetery of the Pacific, September 18, 2015. Service members, veterans, and family members honored and recognized the sacrifices of POWs and remembered those still missing from America's armed conflicts. [U.S. Marine Corps photo by Lance Cpl. Jonathan E. Lopez Cruet]

Serving in Paradise begins in the days when Hawaiian warriors fought with weapons made of wood, stone, and bone. Significant battles, weapons, and tactics of ancient Hawai'i take us back to a time when a warrior prince named Kamehameha came out of the remote north coast of Hawai'i Island to conquer and then consolidate the Islands. His victory of the "Napoleon of the Pacific" at the Battle of Nu'uanu in 1795 is described in detail, where his army fought across the plain that most of Honolulu is built upon today to win the key battle in his decade-long campaign using Western weaponry and battle strategy to achieve victory.

In the late eighteenth and nineteenth centuries, the use of Western weapons—particularly cannon and muskets—solidified the Kamehameha dynasty's rule of the Islands. Foreign governments vied for control of Hawai'i in this era, with warships from Europe and the United States anchoring in Honolulu Harbor. The troops of the monarchy grew in grandeur, at least in obtaining fancy uniforms and learning how to march in parades.

Seven years after the illegal overthrow of the Hawaiian monarchy in 1893, the United States made Hawai'i a territory. This opened the door to the establishment of Army, Air Force, Navy and Marine bases on O'ahu, most significantly the development of a major naval station and shipyard at Pearl Harbor just miles west of Honolulu in the premiere harbor between the West Coast of the United States and Asia.

On December 7, 1941—America's Day of Infamy—the planes of the Imperial Japanese Navy launched a surprise aerial attack on Pearl Harbor, heavily damaging the strategic naval base and placing Hawai'i in the global spotlight. A blow-by-blow account of the day of the Pearl Harbor attack describes both the American and the Japanese sides of the battle.

World War II brought great change to Hawai'i, with over a million soldiers, sailors, Marines, airmen, and coast guardsmen either serving in the Islands or stopping through on the way to battles in the Pacific Theater.

Most significant to Hawai'i's own contribution to the World War II war effort was the sacrifice and bravery of the American men of Japanese Ancestry who served in Europe in the valiant 442nd "Purple Heart Battalion." They struggled to gain acceptance for themselves and their families, some of whom were placed in isolated mainland internment camps.

In the postwar era, Hawai'i served as a staging point for the Korean War, the Vietnam War, the Gulf War, and engagements in the Middle East.

Today at Pearl Harbor and Ford Island, where the bombs of Pearl Harbor fell, respect can be paid at the USS *Arizona* Memorial and one can walk the decks of the USS *Missouri* where Japan surrendered in 1945. ■

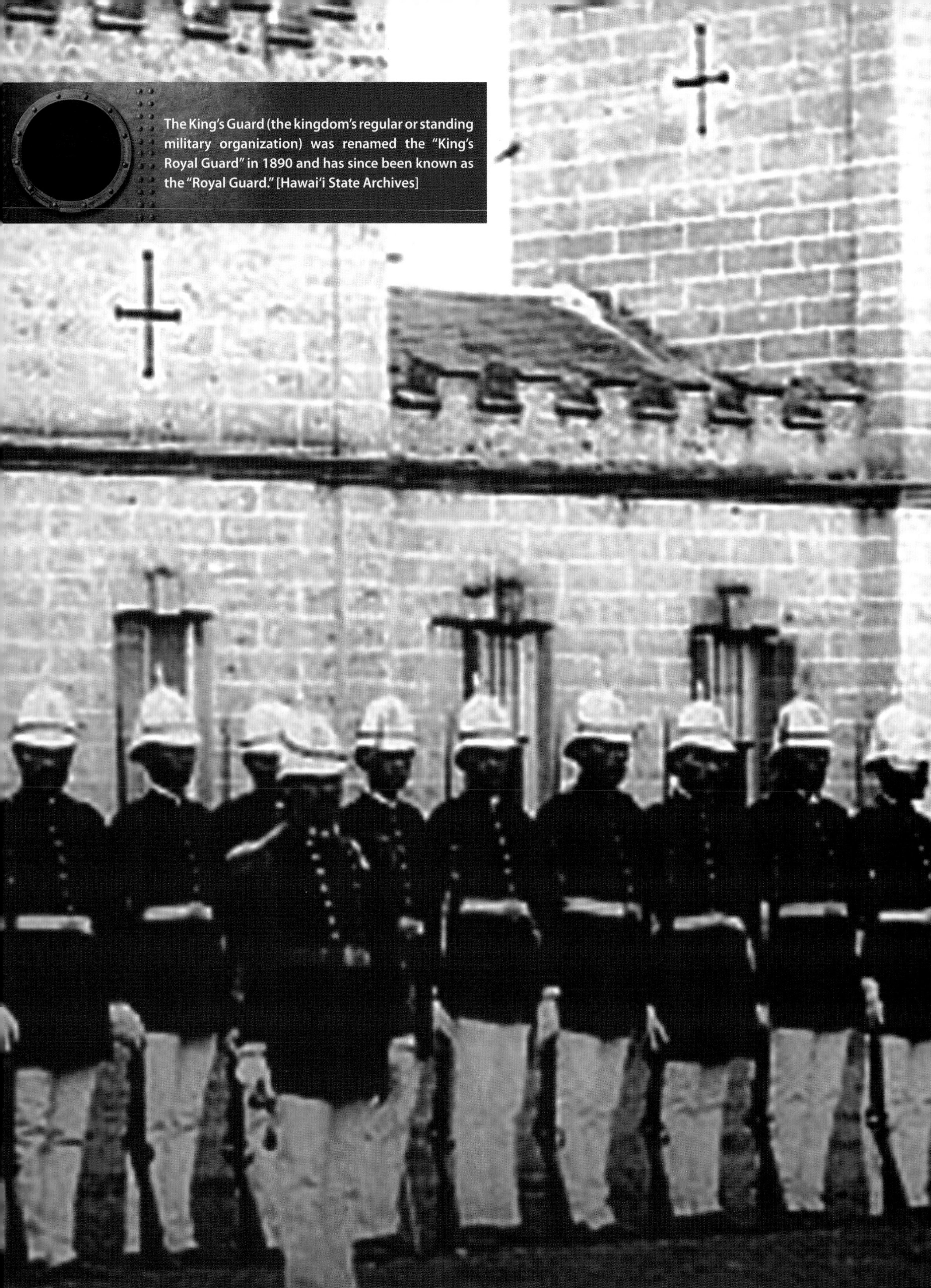

The King's Guard (the kingdom's regular or standing military organization) was renamed the "King's Royal Guard" in 1890 and has since been known as the "Royal Guard." [Hawai'i State Archives]

PROLOGUE
KINGDOM OF HAWAIʻI

THE KINGDOM OF HAWAI'I

A wooden image of the Hawaiian war god Kū stands today on the lawn of the Army's Fort DeRussy. Kū recalls the ancient warrior heritage of Hawai'i that continues today through the U.S. armed forces based on one of the most fortified Islands in the world.

Warriors in ancient Hawai'i were known as koa, the same name as the Islands' tall hardwood koa trees. Select warriors were recruited by chiefs for their strength, physique, bravery, and fighting skills.

The koa trained in close-in combat using daggers known as pāhoa; razor-sharp, shark tooth-edged, handheld blades called leiomano; and lā'au pālau, war clubs with heavy lava rock heads. In battling from a distance, the warriors flung sharp-pointed hardwood spears known as ihe. As a sport, warriors would skillfully parry and catch blunt-tipped spears thrown at them. Elliptically shaped rocks were hurled using slings known as ma'a, a weapon similar to the slingshot used by David to slay Goliath. The prized weapons were handed down from generation to generation.

Warriors trained in the Hawaiian martial art of lua, learning bone-breaking holds in a skill that blended wrestling with spiritual elements of the Hawaiian religion.

The men of the maka'āinana, the commoners, served as a militia. In Hawaiian society the maka'āinana provided food growing taro, the tuber plant grown in rice-paddylike terraces known as lo'i, and fishing using nets onshore and outrigger canoes offshore.

Like the Minutemen of Concord and Lexington, the maka'āinana kept their weapons stowed in the rafters of their thatched homes, ready to go to battle when called to action by the ali'i.

Hawaiian battles of old sometimes focused on one-on-one bouts between champion warriors. Ali'i, the Hawaiian royalty, garbed in distinctive red and yellow-patterned feathered capes, led the warriors and were prize targets. Kāhuna, the priests of the Hawaiian temples, would lead a spiritual attack on the battlefield while standing alongside wooden images of Kū attempting to strike fear in the hearts of the opposing combatants with loud cries. Women and children often observed battles on the sidelines, serving as camp followers for their husbands, fathers, and brothers. At times wahine (female) warriors joined in battle.

Inter- and intra-island wars raged. Epic battles fought within Islands might be compared to those of the American Civil War. The conflicts were often generational in nature.

As in a Shakespearean drama, through bravery and cunning, warrior princes such as Kamehameha could unseat ruling ali'i who ranked higher in the Hawaiian royalty pyramid, usurping to create their own kingdoms.

In January 1778, famed navigator and explorer Captain James Cook of the British Navy anchored his ships, HMS *Discovery* and HMS *Resolution*, off the coast of Waimea, Kaua'i, opening up the Hawaiian Islands to the Western world and introducing modern weaponry to Hawai'i.

Captain Cook died during a skirmish fought between his marines and Hawaiian warriors on a rocky outcrop at Kealakekua Bay on Hawai'i Island in February 1779. Among the warriors attacking the British party attempting to flee to a whaleboat was the tall, strongly built Kamehameha, then a young man. By 1795, the warrior prince, through military savvy and bravery, had become the most powerful chief in all Hawai'i. He decisively won the Battle of Nu'uanu, fought on the plains of today's Honolulu leading to the edge of the Nu'uanu Pali. There hundreds of his opponent's warriors were forced over the edge. This victory brought the main Islands of Hawai'i under his control to form his Kingdom of Hawai'i.

In the era between Cook's death and his victory on O'ahu, Kamehameha rose in stature through his innovative battle tactics and strategic partnerships, his warrior strength and loyalty of his men, marriages to wives from royal families that ruled Islands, and his introduction of Western weapons to the Hawaiian battlefield.

Kamehameha built up his Western armory through deals made with trade ship captains, mostly from New England and Great Britain, who, on their way to the Orient, made provisioning stops in Honolulu Harbor and Kealakekua Bay on Hawaiʻi Island. His armaments included ship cannons and deck rail-mounted swivel guns, muskets and gunpowder, steel knives and daggers.

In his mid-1790s battles, Kamehameha employed British sailors John Young and Isaac Davis, survivors of attacks on their Western ships by Hawaiians. He used them as military advisors, especially in the tactical use of artillery.

Kamehameha ordered hundreds of sleek, double-hulled war canoes, made for speed, to be hewed out of koa trees mostly felled in the mountainsides above Hilo. Known as the peleleu canoe fleet, he planned to use them as troop transports for an invasion of the unconquered leeward Islands of Kauaʻi and Niʻihau. In a 1796 attempt, high winds in the Kauaʻi Channel devastated the fleet, and in 1804 an epidemic, probably of cholera, decimated his troops gathered in Windward Oʻahu. Diplomatic negotiations undertaken in 1810 with Kaumualiʻi, the king of Kauaʻi, backed up with a subtle threat of force, finally gave Kamehameha control of all the Islands.

To display Hawaiʻi's neutrality during the War of 1812 between the U.S. and Great Britain, Kamehameha officially adopted the Hawaiian flag, which combined the British Union Jack and the stripes of the American flag.

In 1817, Kamehameha swiftly removed the Russian American Company from Kauaʻi after a fort was built at Waimea with the help of the Russians. Georg Anton Schäffer, the leader of the Russians, had presented a scheme to King Kaumualiʻi whereby the Russian czar would join forces with him to takeover the Kingdom of Hawaiʻi from Kamehameha. Earlier, in 1815, the Russians began work on a blockhouse overlooking Honolulu Harbor, even raising the Russian flag, emblazoned with the crest of Czar Alexander. Kamehameha recognized the Russian plan as a means to provide the defense he needed for Honolulu Harbor. He soon expanded on the blockhouse, constructing the Honolulu Fort, mounting foreign cannons along its walls. Foreign ships were welcomed with cannon

Honolulu Fort

Interior of Honolulu Fort, Paul Emmert 1853. [Bishop Museum]

Honolulu Fort was established in 1816 in response to an abortive effort to raise the Russian flag over Honolulu harbor. It was a simple rectangular design with twenty-feet thick walls constructed of coral blocks. The fort underwent significant renovations in 1831. By 1853, its numerous guns had become outmoded. It fell briefly to British occupation in 1843 and to the French in 1849. Its troops were often needed to quell disturbances such as the "Sailor's Riot." With the construction of the Bethel police station and Oʻahu Prison, its usefulness ended and it was demolished in 1857. Governor Kekuanaoʻa's office was located in the two-story building to the right.

The King's Guard (the kingdom's regular or standing military organization) was renamed the "King's Royal Guard" in 1890 and has since been known as the "Royal Guard." King Kalākaua was impressed by the professionalism and might of the Prussian Army and modeled his own small force after it. The Hawaiian national flag, which incorporated both British and American stylistic elements, was adopted in the aftermath of the War of 1812 as a symbol of the kingdom's strong ties to both parties and its steadfast commitment to neutrality—particularly important in view of Hawaiʻi's growing naval presence in the Pacific. The eight horizontal stripes stood for each of the major Islands in the archipelago. [Hawaiʻi State Archives]

salutes fired from the fort. The Honolulu Fort was demolished in 1857 and today is recalled by Fort Street in downtown Honolulu.

Following Kamehameha's death at Kailua-Kona in May 1819, control of the Kingdom of Hawaiʻi passed on to his son Liholiho, Kamehameha II. His favorite wife, Kaʻahumanu, reigned as kuhina nui, or prime minister, holding the power behind the throne. Kamehameha's top general, Kalanimoku, led the koa troops.

Soon afterward, with the prompting of Hewahewa, the high priest of the kingdom, the kapu system was overthrown. This set of religious laws was built up over 500 years and dictated how almost every aspect of Hawaiian life was lived. The aliʻi then ordered the destruction of the temples and burning of the wooden images said to serve as reciprocals of the mana (spirit) of the Hawaiian gods.

In reaction to this radical change, the Battle of Kuamoʻo was fought in December 1819 along a coastline strewn with large ʻāʻā lava rocks located just south of Keauhou in the Kona District of Hawaiʻi Island. Kekuaokalani, an aliʻi from the Hāmākua District of Hawaiʻi Island, opposed the overthrow of the kapu system. Using swivel guns mounted on vessels offshore and a superior force of koa on land armed with muskets, the forces of Kamehameha II decimated the invaders. The victory secured the authority of the Kamehameha dynasty over Hawaiʻi and ended the threat of district chiefs attempting to wrest control or break up the Kingdom of Hawaiʻi.

In 1824, the Battle of Wahiawā, fought in southwest Kauaʻi, marked the last major battle fought within the Kingdom of Hawaiʻi. A ragtag army led by Humehume (Prince George Kaumualiʻi), the disgruntled, New England-educated son of Kaumualiʻi, attacked the Russian Fort at Waimea, attempting to regain control of the Island from Kamehameha rule. An alarm raised in Honolulu over the war on Kauaʻi sent an impressive show of force across the channel. The mighty koa soldiers under Kalanimoku soon slaughtered the Kauaʻi upstarts on a plain above Hanapēpē Valley.

The growing importance of Hawaiʻi as the Crossroads of the Pacific in the early nineteenth century drew a steady stream of well-armed foreign warships to Hawaiʻi. Ships from the navies of the United States, Great Britain, France, and Russia all had the firepower to easily take control of Honolulu, which by the 1820s had become the capital of Hawaiʻi. Concurrently, the peace brought by Kamehameha uniting the Islands into one kingdom greatly reduced the need for a rapid response force to fend off uprisings from outlying Island districts. Thus the militia system became a casual home guard service. The mission of the royal army of regulars, the "King's Guards," became more ceremonial than combat ready. The Hawaiian soldiers became a police force when ruckuses were raised in Honolulu and Lahaina, Maui, by the drunken crews of visiting ships reacting to missionary-influenced moral reforms in the ports.

In 1843, during the Paulet Affair, this lack of military strength lost Kamehameha III his sovereignty over the Islands. Lord George Paulet, the pompous captain

The Queen's Royal Guard, circa 1892, posing with the Austrian Uchatius field guns purchased by King Kalākaua during his trip around the world. They are wearing a service dress tunic with turndown collar. Captain Samuel Nowlein is just visible at the center of the photograph wearing a kepi-style hat and a frock jacket. [Hawai'i State Archives]

of a single British Navy man-of-war ship, was able to take over the lightly defended kingdom unopposed. Some 300 men of the King's Guards were disarmed and placed under Paulet's decree by the Hawaiian-manned "Queen's Guard," named in honor of Queen Victoria of Great Britain.

The arrival of Rear Admiral Richard Thomas, the commander-in-chief of the British Navy in the Pacific, soon returned sovereignty over Hawai'i back to Kamehameha III. A grand ceremony was held on a field in Honolulu known today as Thomas Square, located ma kai of the Honolulu Museum of Art. At the Kawaiaha'o Church, the church of the ali'i and the missionaries, the king, in thankfulness for escape from a military takeover, uttered a line likely based on Psalms that became Hawai'i's motto: "Ua mau ke ea o ka 'āina i ka pono" (the life of the land is preserved in righteousness).

As the Victorian era moved along, military units were formed that divided along ethnic lines—Native Hawaiian and foreign "haole" companies. The First Hawaiian Calvary was formed in 1851, enlisting a majority of Native Hawaiians. An infantry company, the First Hawaiian Guard, was made up of foreign residents who started the unit as a gun club. Fancy uniforms imported from Europe added grandeur to their parades.

During the Civil War, the Confederate raider CSS *Shenandoah* roamed the Pacific capturing Northern ships, including whalers from New England. Aboard the *Shenandoah* were twelve Native Hawaiian sailors likely pressed into service after their whale ship was captured. The raids forced Yankee ships to seek refuge in Honolulu Harbor.

Though Kamehameha IV ordered the Kingdom of Hawai'i to remain neutral during the Civil War, a total of about forty men from Hawai'i fought in land battles, most for the Union Army. They were classified as "Sandwich islanders" when signing enlistment rolls. Most prominent was missionary son Gen. Samuel Chapman Armstrong, who was raised on Maui. Armstrong's quick thinking helped turn back Pickett's Charge at the Battle of Gettysburg. This led to a promotion to general and command of a Union regiment made up of black soldiers. Armstrong fought at Hilton Head and in other battles, risking execution by Confederates if captured for serving as an officer leading blacks.

1. Members of the King's Guard and Volunteer Guard companies on parade in front of 'Iolani Palace. Circa 1882. Major David Leleo Kinimaka in command. [Hawai'i State Archives]

2. The funeral procession for Queen Emma, April 25, 1885, marked a high point in the military history of the kingdom, reflecting steady improvement in equipment, organization, morale and enlistment during the early reign of King Kalākaua. The procession was the first major opportunity for the assembled forces to parade in public under arms, many sporting brand new uniforms. The units on parade included: the King's Guard, Leleiohoku Guards, Māmalahoa, Honolulu Rifles, King's Own Volunteer Guards, Queen's Own, and Prince's Own. [Hawai'i State Archives]

A royal barracks for Hawaiian troops serving under the king was constructed in 1866, located on the grounds of today's Hawai'i State Capitol and later moved adjacent to nearby 'Iolani Palace.

The death in 1872 of Lot Kamehameha V ended the succession to the Hawaiian throne of direct descendants of Kamehameha. The Hawai'i Constitution stipulated that once the line of succession was broken, the next ruler must be chosen by a vote of the legislature.

By 1873, the royal troops numbered only forty, mostly serving as guards for the king, the treasury, and a jail. They were disbanded, leaving Hawai'i for the first time with no national army and military affairs to volunteer companies that could be swayed politically. Remaining in service was the Royal Hawaiian Band, formed in 1871.

Armed partisan conflict arose in 1874 with Prince David Kalākaua's election over dowager Queen Emma. Emma was seen by the Hawaiian people as a protector of traditional ways while Kalākaua was viewed as a ruler favoring powerful sugar industry interests. The volunteer militia refused to turn out against the Queen Emma faction. In desperation, the Kingdom of Hawai'i's secretary of war called upon the United States for help in putting down the post-election riot. One hundred and fifty Marines from the warships USS *Tuscarora* and USS *Portsmouth* were landed in Honolulu, plus seventy men from a British warship. The armed foreigners took control of the palace and government buildings.

In the 1880s, Kalākaua, under the influence of wily prime minister Walter Murray Gibson, pictured Hawai'i

as becoming a major power in a federation of Pacific Island nations. While on a European tour, the king began a military buildup, purchasing state-of-the-art Austrian artillery pieces and ordering uniforms modeled upon those of the Prussian Army. Modern Winchester rifles and Gatling guns were bought. He built up the King's Guard, creating a small standing army, and gathered a volunteer 200-man reserve.

Opposing the king were the "Annexationists," a political faction aligned with the sugar planters across the Islands and big business interests in Honolulu. They favored Hawai'i becoming a territory of the United States. To counter Kalākaua's growing military might, the Annexationists formed the Honolulu Rifles, a part military and part social club organization. The Rifles paraded in 1885, wearing dark blue uniforms very similar to the ones worn by the U.S. Army regulars. In 1887, the Rifles had a standoff with the King's Guard over control of government buildings during a riot when a secret organization dubbed the "Hawaiian League" began pushing constitutional reform. Kalākaua apparently decided to avoid an armed conflict between the factions which he feared might again bring in troops from foreign warships. He signed a "Bayonet Constitution" that weakened his hold on power. The Hawaiian government at this time opened up Pearl Harbor to the U.S. War Department in exchange for continuing to remove tariffs on imports of Hawaiian sugar and other products.

In 1889, Native Hawaiian Robert Wilcox returned from a kingdom-supported term of studying artillery in Italy. The young part-Hawaiian officer decided to march on the palace to seize the government's arsenal hoping to institute a new constitution returning power to the monarchy. Wilcox raised a company of eighty poorly armed "Patriots," who were confronted by the Rifles and kept out of the palace grounds by the King's Guard. Marines from the USS *Adams* landed and guarded the American Legation offices in downtown Honolulu.

On the afternoon of January 17, 1893, the Provisional Government of Hawai'i was declared on the back steps of Ali'iolani Hale. Two days later, all foreign nations represented in the Islands had recognized this new government. Its Executive Council consisted of Sanford B. Dole, President; James A. King, Minister of the Interior; William O. Smith, Attorney General; and Peter C. Jones, Minister of Finance. [Hawai'i State Archives]

Sharpshooters and dynamite blasts broke up the revolt and eight of Wilcox's men were killed.

Kalākaua died in early 1891, his funeral procession led by the Royal Hawaiian Band and the King's Royal Guard, which had been reduced to about sixty men.

Queen Lili'uokalani became ruler and faced a crisis in November 1892 when she attempted to institute a new pro-monarchy constitution. America's representative in Hawai'i, John L. Stevens, used her actions as an excuse to land some 160 Marines from the USS *Boston* anchored in Honolulu Harbor. The Marines marched through downtown Honolulu and took up a post near the Queen's 'Iolani Palace. The action, which still remains controversial in the twenty-first century, led to the overthrow of the Kingdom of Hawai'i and the establishment of an Annexationist-led Provisional Government.

Hawai'i was annexed by the United States in 1898 and became a territory in 1900, opening the door for a full contingent of military bases across O'ahu. ■

THE USS *BOSTON*

On the evening of January 16, 1893, troops of the USS *Boston* landed. They were quartered at the Arlington Hotel in downtown Honolulu, the former home of Princess Bernice Pauahi Bishop. The hotel became known as "Camp Boston" when martial law was declared by the provisional government. The 162 soldiers were supposedly only to protect American property and lives during anticipated political upheavals. Queen Lili'uokalani protested that a majority of the troops were quartered directly across from Ali'iōlani Hale, the government building almost across from 'Iolani Palace, an area where no Americans resided or owned property. The troops were in an excellent position, however, to defend the leaders of the revolution who were about to declare a provisional government. Many to this day believe that if the soldiers had not landed, the overthrow of the monarchy and the subsequent Provisional Government would not have happened. [Hawai'i State Archives]

One hundred and sixty-two Marines and sailors from the cruiser USS *Boston* landed at the foot of Nuʻuanu Avenue in Honolulu on the afternoon of January 16, 1893. To this day, the action remains a controversial and contentious event in a chain of circumstances that led to the overthrow of the Kingdom of Hawaiʻi and the annexation of the Islands by the United States.

By early 1893, Queen Lydia Liliʻuokalani had reigned less than two years, facing trouble from the start. Control of the Hawaiian government was at stake, with the traditional ruler of Hawaiʻi and her supporters seeking to bolster the monarchy through instituting a new constitution. Opposing the queen's actions were the powerful sugar industry and community leaders who supported annexation to the United States as the best course for Hawaiʻi's interests, and who saw Liliʻuokalani as an ineffective ruler. The legislative session had run on for extra months, the queen making four changes to her ruling ministry. This conflict came to a head on January 14, the closing day of the legislature, when Liliʻuokalani proposed a new constitution that supported a strong, monarchy form of government. Her supporters rallied behind her, gathering at ʻIolani Palace alongside Kingdom of Hawaiʻi troops. At

1. On the evening of January 16, 1893, troops of the USS *Boston* landed illegally. They are pictured here at "Camp Boston" with their Gatling guns. [Bishop Museum]

2. The American military troops that landed on January 16, 1893 were later quartered at the Arlington Hotel in downtown Honolulu. The former home of Princess Bernice Pauahi Bishop, the hotel became known as "Camp Boston" when martial law was declared by the Provisional Government. [Hawai'i State Archives]

Queen Lili'uokalani's Household Guard is disbanded at the Royal Barracks, then located on the site of today's Hawai'i State Capitol, by Col. J. H. Soper, commanding the Provisional Government forces in January, 1893, following the overthrow of the Hawaiian monarchy. The Hawaiian troops stacked their arms, turned over their equipment, and listened to a "By Authority" notice, which ended the rule of the monarchy. [Hawai'i State Archives]

the last minute, her cabinet opposed the new constitution, debating with the queen. She announced that her proclamation would be delayed, an action her opposition used as an excuse to form a Committee of Safety, planning to end the long rule of the Hawaiian monarchy. A meeting was held by the committee on January 16, and a provisional government was formed. Reorganizing began of the 1,500-man Honolulu Rifles, a volunteer military company that had been disbanded in 1889 after an insurrection against the monarchy. As this crisis developed, the USS *Boston* sailed for Honolulu Harbor from an anchorage in Hilo Harbor, where the Navy ship had been at port for some time. The ship had departed from New York in October 1891 for the Pacific, sailing around the Horn for San Francisco and cruising to Hawaiʻi in August 1892.

The Committee of Safety requested the U.S. minister to the Kingdom of Hawaiʻi, John L. Stevens, to land Marines from the *Boston*. Stevens replied that Captain Wiltse of the *Boston* had been given orders to land a battalion to maintain law and order in Honolulu to protect the interests of its American residents and properties. The sailors and Marines from the *Boston*, under orders of neutrality, marched toward ʻIolani Palace, with officers stationing troops at the U.S. Consulate at Merchant Street and the U.S. legation at School Street. The remainder marched down King Street as a show of force, quartering that night at Arion Hall, across from ʻIolani Palace. The men from the *Boston* never fired a shot nor entered the palace grounds, but the threat posed by their presence checked the royalist forces supporting Liliʻuokalani. The queen, wishing to avoid an armed conflict, ordered her armed Royal Guard to surrender, and the Honolulu Rifles took control of government buildings.

On January 17, a provisional government led by Sanford Ballard Dole of the Committee of Safety issued a proclamation declaring the dissolution of the Kingdom of Hawaiʻi and plans for a "union with the United States of America."

The *Boston* men moved two days later, billeting at the Arlington Hotel, about 300 yards down King Street west of the palace. They renamed the facility "Camp Boston." Stevens rented the facility from annexation supporter Charles Reed Bishop. That evening the sailors and Marines marched to the palace in a dress parade.

The morning of February 1, the company marched to the Government Building across King Street from the palace, where they formed up and stood at attention before members of the Provisional Government standing on the steps of the building. At 11 a.m., a proclamation signed by Stevens was read aloud announcing that the Hawaiian Islands were now a protectorate of the United States. The Hawaiian flag was lowered and the American flag raised, and the sound of a twenty-one-gun salute fired from the *Boston* boomed up from Honolulu Harbor.

The American flag was soon lowered upon order from Washington, D.C., and the Provisional Government became the Republic of Hawaiʻi in 1894. Annexation came in 1898, and through the Organic Act, the Territory of Hawaiʻi was formed in 1900. Liliʻuokalani was placed under house arrest for nine months in Honolulu in 1895 following an unsuccessful attempt to restore the monarchy. In Liliʻuokalani's appeals to the United States to restore her throne, she pointed to the landing of the Marines and sailors from the *Boston* as the key action in the usurption of her kingdom. ■

BATTLE OF NU'UANU

The culminating battle of Kamehameha's thirteen-year struggle to unite the Islands was in fought 1795. The battle began along the plain upon which much of Honolulu sits today. The warrior chief's well-prepared invasion force routed the allied forces of O'ahu, Maui, and Kaua'i up Nu'uanu Valley to face certain defeat atop a 1,200-foot precipice. After the battle, only the Islands of Kaua'i and Ni'ihau remained beyond Kamehameha's immediate grasp. [*The Battle at Nu'uanu Pali* © 2009 Herb Kawainui Kāne]

Honolulu was once the scene of a great battle fought by 25,000 Hawaiian warriors. Few today realize that on a fateful hot day in May 1795, the roar of cannons, the shrill yells of combatants, and the groans of dying warriors echoed over a battlefield now covered by urban buildings, highways, and streets.

The epic conflict determined Hawai'i's future. Kamehameha's victory over Kalanikupule, ruler of O'ahu, brought him control of all the Hawaiian Islands, except leeward Kaua'i and Ni'ihau.

From the overlook at Punchbowl Crater, one can picture the extent of the battle. Along the coast, hundreds of Kamehameha's double-hulled canoe fleet lay beached in a line four miles long, stretching from Wai'alae Beach to the shore below Lē'ahi (Diamond Head) to Waikīkī Beach. The armada, originating from Hawai'i Island (the Big Island), transported some 10,000 warriors across the Moloka'i Channel.

The Battle of Nu'uanu culminated Kamehameha's quest begun in the 1780s to conquer and unify the windward Hawaiian Islands. A Kaua'i prophet's advice had been followed in building up Pu'ukoholā Heiau overlooking Kawaihae Bay on the leeward shore of Hawai'i Island. There Kamehameha's officers slew

Keōua, his rival for control of Hawaiʻi Island, solidifying his rule from his birthplace at ʻUpolu Point in Kohala on the north tip of the Island to the southernmost district of Kaʻū.

British naval captain George Vancouver, making several voyages to Hawaiʻi in the early 1790s, served as an advisor to Kamehameha on Western battle strategies and tactics.

British sailors John Young and Isaac Davis, along with a handful of other Western men with military experience, manned ship cannons for Kamehameha, some of the weapons mounted on double hulled canoes, others on schooners and others kept on land.

Kamehameha saw an opening when the powerful Maui and Oʻahu ruler, Kahekili, died and his lands were divided between Kaʻeo, who was aligned with Kauaʻi through marriage, and his son Kalanikupule. Kalanikupule was heir to Kahekili's Maui dynasty and had faced Kamehameha in the Battle of ʻĪao Valley, where ʻĪao Stream was said to have run blood red.

In November 1794, Kaʻeo led his men from Waiʻanae in west Oʻahu to ʻAiea, to a plain at the north and east banks of Pearl Harbor. A British sea captain provided Kalanikupule with a small boat armed with a cannon. The opposing forces built up near Pearl Harbor and in December 1794, with the help of cannon fire, Kalanikupule routed his opponent, but losses of warriors during the battle weakened his army.

This opened up an opportunity for Kamehameha to sweep west and conquer Maui, Molokaʻi, and then Oʻahu, a campaign begun in February 1795. In November 1794, the British trading ship *Butterworth,* commanded by Captain Brown, became the first to anchor in Honolulu Harbor. The discovery of a safe anchorage in mid-Pacific with room for many ships along the trade route between the Pacific Northwest and China made Honolulu the central port of the Hawaiian Islands and Oʻahu, the key Island in Kamehameha's building of the Kingdom of Hawaiʻi.

Kalanikupule and his chiefs turned to subterfuge in anticipating the invasion by Kamehameha. The key to defeating the invader was using the firepower of foreign ships to smash at sea the peleleu fleet and keeping any escaping canoes from landing on Oʻahu beaches. Beyond that, the armed ships could lead them to retaking Maui and then attacking the stronghold of Kamehameha on Hawaiʻi Island. To accomplish that, on January 1, 1795, Kalanikupule sent warriors to seize the merchant ships *Jackall* and *Prince Lee Boo* anchored in Honolulu Harbor. The ship captains were killed, but at sea the Western crews surprised their captors, retaking the ships and sending Kalanikupule back in a boat to the beach where he then fled the Island. Kalanikupule might have won the Battle of Nuʻuanu had he kept control of the *Jackall* and the *Prince Lee Boo.*

In spring 1795, crossing the ʻAlenuihāhā Channel and landing on Maui, Kamehameha's warriors met little resistance. The warriors of Kalanikupule fled the Island for Oʻahu to consolidate and give battle. The army of Kamehameha raided Lāhainā for supplies, leaving the people of West Maui in fear of retribution should they mount a revolt against his rule. The peleleu fleet then sailed to Molokaʻi, landing at Kaunakakai, easily taking control of the Island.

With reports indicating Kamehameha's proceeding march to Oʻahu, Kalanikupule ordered the building of defenses near Punchbowl Crater and up Nuʻuanu Valley.

On Molokaʻi, the Kaʻū chief Kaʻiana defected from Kamehameha after failing to be invited to a meeting of generals preparing a battle plan for the invasion of Oʻahu. Kaʻiana had studied Chinese military tactics during a voyage to Canton aboard a Western trading ship. The outspoken warrior's boasts of his own military prowess became a threat to Kamehameha, continuing the age-old conflict between rulers of the southern districts of Hawaiʻi Island and its central and northern districts.

Secretly, Kaʻiana and his brother Nahiolea gathered their troops and crossed the Molokaʻi Channel aboard canoes, landing on Windward Oʻahu beaches. Gathering his men, Kaʻiana led them up to the Pali, cutting through the wide notch in the Koʻolaus from the windward side, and joined forces with Kalanikupule's army.

The first line of defense for the army of Kalanikupule lay ma uka (inland) of Punchbowl Crater behind rock walls previously built as battlements. Kamehameha

split his 16,000-warrior army in two, sending one force directly at the O'ahu lines, while flanking the O'ahu defenders above them to a place known at La'imi, near today's O'ahu Country Club and Queen Emma's Summer Palace. He brought up cannon to shell La'imi, and, foreseeing the direction of the battle, Kamehameha sent a detachment to overrun the cannon emplacements set up in the heights of Nu'uanu Valley.

At La'imi, Ka'iana led a company dug in on a steep hill looking down on the invaders. The position would have been a strong one in the days of close-in Hawaiian battles, when victory would have been determined by warriors skilled in spear and pike fighting and in the martial art of lua. But now Western cannon, able to fire long range, were in the fore. An account of the battle has Kamehameha's loyal English sailor John Young aiming a cannon at Ka'iana's position, smashing the rock-wall barricade, fatally wounding Ka'iana and quickly ending the skirmish.

With their generals facing chaos in the face of the "red-mouth" cannon of Kamehameaha, Kalanikupule's troops retreated up Nu'uanu Valley.

Three notches had been cut into the ridge flanking the Pali, and Kalanikupule's last-ditch plan was to fire down the valley at the invading troops. Kamehameha countered by attacking from behind the ridge.

At the Pali Lookout, the O'ahu warriors literally had their backs to the wall, with Kamehameha's men charging their front and behind them a sheer drop of 500 feet down the rugged Pali cliff dropoff. Some scattered up into the Ko'olaus, while over 400 warriors chose either to leap rather than be captured or to be forcibly pushed over the Pali, falling down to their deaths, striking the valley floor below.

Their "whitened bones long bore witness to battle," a late-nineteenth-century account notes. While working on what is known today as the Old Pali Road, the Whitehouse and Wilson engineering firm construction workers discovered some 800 skulls and other human bones on the valley floor below the Pali Lookout. The remains were buried under tons of crushed rocks dumped over the side of road cuts blasted out during the Pali Road construction.

Aftermath

In the seasons following the Battle of Nu'uanu, the people of O'ahu suffered greatly from sorrow and famine due to the loss of so many men who once worked taro fields and fished the shoreline to feed their families. The lands of O'ahu were taken by Kamehameha, and ownership was given to ali'i loyal to him.

Kalanikupule spent several months on the run in the wilderness forest of the Ko'olau Mountains and down to the 'Ewa District. He was captured in the upper section of Waipi'o, the valley located between Pearl City and Wahiawā. The vanquished chief was killed and his body brought to Kamehameha who placed it on the altar of a heiau in Moanalua Valley, where it was burnt as a sacrifice to Kamehameha's personal war god, Kūkā'ilimoku.

To solidify his control of O'ahu, Kamehameha spent a year on the Island. The powerful ruler continued to look west towards Kaua'i and Ni'ihau, the last two major Islands outside his kingdom. At Waikīkī, with a headquarters set up on the site of today's Royal Hawaiian Hotel, Kamehameha consolidated his beached peleleu fleet in preparation for an attack on the leeward Islands located some 70 miles across the Kaua'i Channel.

In April 1796, Kamehameha's fleet departed from the leeward coast of Wai'anae, paddling out in the wind shadow of Mount Ka'ala northwest toward Kaua'i. High winds and waves in the treacherous channel swamped many of the sleek war canoes, drowning his warriors and halting the invasion.

The Battle of Nu'uanu became a turning point in Hawaiian history as the last significant battle fought by Kamehameha in establishing his Kingdom of Hawai'i. O'ahu became the center of interaction with Western traders sailing to Hawai'i in the years following the battle overshadowing Kealakekua for good and laying the roots for the development of Honolulu as the capital of the Hawaiian Islands. ■

The construction of a dry dock at Pearl Harbor was essential to the long-range plan of making Hawai'i the center of operations for the U.S. Navy's Pacific fleet. On August 21, 1919, the dry dock was finally opened with an elaborate ceremony. [National Archives]

TERRITORIAL
DAYS
1900–1941

THE SPANISH-AMERICAN WAR

U.S. troops heading to a lū'au on the grounds of 'Iolani Palace in 1898. [*Overland Monthly Magazine*, No. 191, Vol XXXII, 1898]

The Spanish-American War of 1898 brought far-reaching changes to Hawai'i. American troops garrisoned at Camp McKinley near Diamond Head began the permanent presence of the U.S. military in the Islands. Jingoism was generated by the defeat in Manila of the Pacific Squadron of Spain by the U.S. Asiatic Squadron led by Commodore Dewey. This persuaded Atlantic Ocean–minded Congress, and the American public, of the necessity of building a significant naval base on O'ahu at the Crossroads of the Pacific.

President William McKinley signed a bill on July 7, 1898, annexing the Hawaiian Islands, completing their transition from a sovereign kingdom to a territory of the United States. War was declared against Spain in April 1898 over the sinking of the battleship *Maine* in Cuba. Uncertainty over Dewey's situation in Manila caused the War Department to order the rapid transport of 15,000 soldiers to relieve him, with plans to seize Manila and all of the Philippines. This brought a flood of troops passing through Honolulu. Most landed for only a few days during coaling stops at Honolulu Harbor by convoys of commercial transport ships chartered to carry them to the Philippines.

The first troops to arrive received a grand greeting, with red, white, and blue bunting and American flags decorating Honolulu and an invite to a huge lū'au on the grounds of 'Iolani Palace, then known at the Executive Building of the Republic of Hawai'i. Princess Ka'iulani, the heir to the Hawaiian throne, entertained officers at 'Āinahau, her family's gracious estate at Waikīkī.

In August 1898, concurrently with the declaration of annexation and the lowering of the Hawaiian flag at 'Iolani Palace, the first American troops to be billeted in Hawai'i arrived. The First New York Volunteers and the Engineer Volunteers, a company drawn from across the United States, marched four miles from Honolulu Harbor to the Kapi'olani Park racetrack located near Waikīkī and below the west slope of Diamond Head. There they garrisoned at Camp McKinley, a field of tents named for the president who sent them to Hawai'i.

A warm greeting for the troops came from all of Honolulu's people—from Native Hawaiians to the missionariy families, sugar planters to Chinese and Japanese immigrants—with opposition to the annexation set aside during days of military glory. At Camp McKinley, they found sparse grass fields encrusted with sharp lava rocks and pitched their canvas Army tents amidst stands of thorny kiawe trees. Marching drills were trimmed to two hours while they acclimated to the warm climate. Scorpions and centipedes pestered them. The troops dipped into their monthly pay of just over $15.00 to buy local foods to supplement a sparse diet of bread, water, and Army meat, and they were warned they might die if they ate Hawaiian fruit.

Camp Otis, a second nearby billet, was built in the open space of Kapi'olani Park fairgrounds, closer to the beach. Work parties ordered to do fatigue duty dug trenches, built roads, and drained swampy fields near Waikīkī Beach. The first group of Red Cross workers organized in Hawai'i served the troops, and Honolulu residents held Thanksgiving and Christmas dinners for them.

Work on permanent barracks at Waikīkī took place near the future site of Fort DeRussy, with Camp

The United States wasted no time consolidating their power in the Islands. Four days after annexation, the 1st New York Volunteer Infantry and the U.S. Volunteer Engineers arrived in Honolulu. 1, 2. The New Yorkers, photographed at their official posting, Camp McKinley in Kapi'olani Park spent several months in the Islands before returning to the mainland. 3. Buena Vista, a private home in Nu'uanu Valley, was used as a hospital for them. When Camp McKinley was vacated the military paid over three thousand dollars to repair damage to the grounds. [U.S. Army Museum of Hawai'i]

McKinley deactivated in 1904. On occasion, hundreds of troops from the Hawai'i National Guard trained alongside the U.S. troops.

Though the Spanish-American War officially ended in August 1898, American troops and naval vessels continued to port in Honolulu in 1899 en route to fighting in the Philippines Insurrection that followed the armistice with Spain. The ships, almost all lacking enough storage room for the hundreds of tons of coal burned crossing the Pacific, loaded coal at a makeshift Navy yard set up in Honolulu Harbor. This strategic necessity, put in the spotlight by the Spanish-American War, led to the passage of bills in Congress funding the development of Pearl Harbor as a major naval base. The United States was becoming a world military and economic power, with Hawai'i now a key site in defense of the nation. ■

THE U.S. MILITARY SETS UP CAMP

After annexation, the United States military moved swiftly to transform the Islands into a Western defense perimeter for the expanding U.S. presence in Asia. Parades and reviews were frequent, as seen in this photo of cavalry marching in downtown Honolulu. [Hawai'i State Archives]

The Building of the Big Bases

From a military perspective, Hawai'i's strategic location had long made the Islands a desirable acquisition for the United States. Ships of the U.S. Navy regularly called throughout the nineteenth century, and the Navy saw Pearl Harbor as a potential base. Annexation became more urgent when it was suddenly recognized that Hawai'i was an important halfway point for refreshing troops headed to the Philippines during the Spanish-American War and the ensuing nationalist insurrections. Negotiations proceeded at full speed and American soldiers were already on their way from California, arriving just four days after the official annexation date of August 12, 1898.

The Army. The first U.S. Army encampment was set up at a site in Kapi'olani Park when infantry and engineer elements paused here en route to the Philippines. Called Camp McKinley, it was the only military establishment in the territory until 1907, when Fort Shafter was built.

With annexation, the Army was faced with the task of defending the new territory. In 1908, work was begun on a new major military post on the Leilehua plateau of central O'ahu. This post was named Schofield Barracks to honor Civil War Lt. Gen. John M. Schofield, who had earlier visited Hawai'i and recommended the acquisition of Pearl Harbor for the Navy. Wheeler Field, at the south end of Schofield, was established by the Army Air Corps in 1922. Construction of Hickam Field began in 1935. Later, the Army Air Corps became a separate branch of service, the Air Force.

The Navy. The first U.S. Navy ship to visit Hawai'i anchored in Honolulu Harbor in 1826. Some twenty-five years before annexation, the Navy built a coaling station in Honolulu. Construction of the giant Pearl Harbor naval complex began in 1909 and in 1911 the USS *California* became the first U.S. warship to enter Pearl Harbor.

The Marines. The Marine Corps first moved into Pearl Harbor barracks in 1923. In 1953 the former Naval Air Station at Kāne'ohe was recommissioned as a Marine Corps Air Station.

The Coast Guard. Coast Guard cutters have been patrolling Hawaiian waters since the Spanish-American War. Today the Hawai'i-based Coast Guard supervises a vast area of the central Pacific, ranging as far as Alaska and Samoa.

World War I. Hawai'i and the military forces stationed here played a minor part in the affairs of World War I. Nine German naval vessels were seized upon the outbreak of hostilities between Germany and the U.S. The vessels had previously sought sanctuary in Hawai'i from the Japanese Navy in 1914 during America's period of neutrality.

World War II and Afterwards. By the late 1930s it became obvious that the U.S. and Japan would clash in the Pacific, and the military establishment in Hawai'i grew larger each year. After the December 7, 1941, Pearl Harbor surprise attack, martial law was declared. Hawai'i remained under military rule until October 19, 1944. Life for Island residents under martial law was difficult. Most normal civil rights were suspended, and curfews and restrictions were imposed. The press was heavily censored, especially the two Japanese American dailies that were allowed to continue printing. Wages of all workers were frozen and work absenteeism was punishable by jail sentence. Some have argued that there was no real need for such a lengthy period of military control.

During the Korean and Vietnam conflicts, the Islands served as a staging area as well as a popular rest and recuperation center. Today, defense is a major industry in Hawai'i. With the U.S. withdrawing from key Asian bases and the Asian Theater remaining a risk area, Hawai'i is as important as ever as a military base. ■

Sergeant Alex Akita of Honomu's National Guard unit, the 299th Infantry, sits in the front row, holding the unit plaque. Note the small cannon and water-cooled machine gun. After Pearl Harbor, Japanese Americans were asked to leave the Guard. Many of them later found their way into military units such as the much-decorated Japanese American 442nd Regimental Combat Team. 1929. [Yugawa Family Collection]

Schofield Barracks

The largest American military base in the United States was Schofield Barracks, which encompassed 14,400 acres in the center of the Island of O'ahu. Established in 1909, Schofield Barracks was home to the Hawaiian Division of the United States Army, which during the 1930s had been reinforced to a strength of over 20,000 soldiers. In addition to Schofield Barracks, the Hawaiian Division consisted of airbases at Wheeler Field at Wahiawā, Luke Field on Ford Island at Pearl Harbor, and a coastal and harbor defense system at Fort DeRussy, Fort Ruger and Fort Armstrong. U.S. troops were stationed at the entrance to Pearl Harbor at Fort Kamehameha, and the entire operations of the Hawaiian Department were headquartered at Fort Shafter. Tripler General Hospital, located at Fort Shafter, about three miles from downtown Honolulu, had a 300-bed capacity, which in an emergency could be enlarged to 600 beds. With the U.S. Army's Hawaiian Division under General Walter C. Short and the Pacific Fleet of the United States Navy at Pearl Harbor under Admiral Husband E. Kimmel, the military believed, in 1941, that America's fist in the Pacific was invincible.

Pictured above and opposite: aerial of Schofield Barracks; below is a 1923 aerial view of Wheeler Field next to Schofield Barracks as seen from the northwest. [All photos Hawai'i State Archives]

After annexation, the United States military moved swiftly to transform the Islands into a Western defense perimeter for the expanding American presence in Asia.

1.The former Royal Barracks of the Hawaiian Kingdom became the backdrop for a photograph of U.S. soldiers standing at attention in downtown Honolulu.

2. Parades and reviews were frequent, as seen in this photo of a special military show at Kapi'olani Park.

3. Fort Ruger served as the headquarters of the Harbor Defenses of Honolulu, and in 1909 a Coast Artillery post was established on the slopes of Diamond Head, with officers' housing in simple cottages. Fort DeRussy was also founded in 1909, and tents were erected on the Waikīkī grounds of former private residences bought by the U.S. government. As headquarters of the Hawaiian Separate Coast Artillery Brigade, Fort DeRussy boasted Battery Randolph with two massive "disappearing" guns positioned to protect the western coastline of O'ahu. Eventually the Hawaiian Division was headquartered at Schofield Barracks, encompassing over 14,000 acres in central O'ahu. During the 1920s and 1930s as tensions mounted in Europe and Asia, U.S. military forces in Hawai'i increased and troops in the streets of Honolulu were a common sight. "The Paradise of the Pacific is armed!" enthused a 1914 Hawai'i guidebook. "Oahu will soon be a veritable Gibraltar." [2, Hawai'i State Archives; 1, 3, Bishop Museum]

THE DEVELOPMENT OF PEARL HARBOR

Pearl Harbor, the hub of the U.S. Navy in the Pacific, burst into global importance on December 7, 1941, the "Day of Infamy," when Imperial Japanese Navy pilots bombed the base, leading to America's involvement in World War II.

Almost a century earlier, the development of Pearl Harbor began when a Navy officer recognized the strategic importance of Pearl Harbor's protected waters. It was already known that Honolulu Harbor offered the best anchorage in the vast North Pacific between the West Coast of the United States and Asia. But Lt. I. W. Curtis, aboard the USS *Constitution*—"Old Ironsides"—noted in an 1846 communication to the Kingdom of Hawai'i that the broad, deep, protected waters of the Hawaiian fishing ground to the west of Honolulu known as Pu'uloa could provide anchorage for many more ships than Honolulu Harbor. The waterway would make for an excellent naval base, he concluded.

Following the Civil War, in 1872, Honolulu newspaper publisher and postmaster Henry Whitney, the son of Kaua'i missionaries, wrote an editorial proposing a solution to the pressing need for support of Hawai'i's stalled sugar growing industry. Whitney called for leasing Pearl Harbor to the United States for fifty years in exchange for the dropping of tariffs on Kingdom of Hawai'i sugar exported to America. The publication of Whitney's opinion piece coincided with a covert visit to Hawai'i by Maj. Gen. John Schofield, the namesake of the U.S. Army's Schofield Barracks at Wahiawā. While posing as vacationers, Schofield and a fellow officer were instead scouting the defensive capabilities of Kingdom of Hawai'i ports along O'ahu's coastline. Seeing that steamships were eclipsing sail-powered frigates in the U.S. fleet, Schofield reported that the United States should build a naval station in Hawai'i. A coaling and repair station should be built to service visiting American Navy and merchant ships. Schofield noted that a shallow coral shelf blocking the entrance to Pearl Harbor would need to be blasted away. Once the harbor mouth of the almost landlocked waterway provided entrance for deep-draft warships, Pearl Harbor would be a port of great strategic value.

View of Pearl Harbor from the entrance. [Hawaiian Gazette Co., 1890]

In 1874, newly elected King Kalākaua visited Washington, D.C., to propose a treaty that would allow unrefined Hawaiian sugar and other local products to enter the United States duty free in exchange for American products entering Hawai'i duty free. This Reciprocity Treaty was signed in 1876 and was to last seven years. By 1883, the Hawaiian sugar industry took off, expanding across all the Islands. However, in the halls of Congress complaints echoed that the United States was getting the short end of the deal. To extend the Reciprocity Treaty for seven more years, the Kingdom of Hawai'i must give an exclusive right to the United States to enter Pearl Harbor. There a coaling and repair station for American vessels would be built and used only for a limited period of time. This concession was granted by King Kalākaua, who faced opposition from Native Hawaiians opposed to allowing a foreign nation inroads into the Kingdom of Hawai'i.

In 1898, the outbreak of the Spanish-American War led to the United States expanding its military

1. The U.S. annexation of the Hawaiian Islands in 1898 had been justified by its supporters as a necessary strategy for the protection of American interests in the Pacific against the possible growing presence of Japan. By establishing a naval base at Pearl Harbor, these strategists urged, the United States would have a powerful dominion over the future of the Pacific region. The construction of a dry dock at Pearl Harbor was essential to the long-range plan of making Hawai'i the center of operations for the U.S. Navy's Pacific fleet. On August 21, 1919, the dry dock was finally opened with an elaborate ceremony. "Pearl Harbor," wrote a prophetic editor of one of the Honolulu newspapers a few years earlier, "is going to settle the destiny of the world." [National Archives]

2. Just as drydock construction was on the verge of completion, the entire structure collapsed into the harbor. [Hawaiian Legacy Archives]

A AIDS ENGINEERS TO COMPLETE
PEARL HARBOR DRY DOCK

Shark God of
h Seas appeased

operations across the entire Pacific, from California to Guam and the Philippines. This led to Pearl Harbor and Honolulu becoming the hub of Pacific naval operations. The annexation of Hawai'i in 1898 was a major step toward the Islands becoming a territory of the United States in 1900, opening a floodgate of federal military funding for the Islands. These developments led to Congress approving the acquisition of land along the coast of Pearl Harbor for a permanent naval station and for the dredging of the shallow channel. A site for a Navy yard on the east side of the harbor was acquired, as was the southeast coast of Ford Island, and dredging of the channel and sections of the harbor began.

In January 1905, the gunboat USS *Petrel* motored into the main loch of the harbor. In 1908, Congress authorized the secretary of the Navy to create a major naval base at Pearl Harbor. Given priority were construction of a drydock and dredging of the ship channel and lochs to "admit the largest ships." Machine shops and supply warehouses were also included in the $3 million budget. The cruiser USS *California,* the flagship of the Pacific fleet and the biggest ship in Navy service, entered the newly dredged Pearl Harbor Channel, becoming the first large Navy ship to pass into the deep waters of the inner harbor.

Setbacks occurred as the base at Pearl Harbor developed, most notably the sudden collapse of Dry Dock No. 1 in February 1913. About a thousand pilings gave way, sounding like tons of gunpowder going off according to firsthand reports. An official Navy report cited the implosion of the drydock, about three football fields long, as the "naval disaster of the year." The cause was faulty piling and foundation design. No one was killed or injured in the collapse, though some

workers narrowly escaped when they noticed the floor of the foundation dug for the drydock rising from the bottom.

Building atop the underwater cavern where the legendary Hawaiian shark god Ka'aupahau lived was the actual cause of the drydock's collapse according to local construction workers laboring at the project. They blamed a lack of respect for Hawaiian traditions as the source of the spectacular collapse that destroyed four years of work. A Hawaiian blessing preceded the second attempt at building, and the work moved along, with the $5 million drydock dedicated by Secretary of the Navy, Josephus Daniels, in August 1919.

The work on the drydock and building of naval base facilities brought in many men from the mainland United States who worked alongside local men. The good-paying construction jobs established Pearl Harbor and its shipyard as a key employer in Hawai'i's economy. Alongside the drydock, the workers built machine shops, office buildings, electric shops, oil tanks and power plants, a wireless radio facility beaming out a few hundred miles, housing, a Marine barracks, recreation facilities, and a magazine storing shells, bombs, and mines.

The naval station established in the early 1900s at Honolulu Harbor moved to its new quarters in Pearl Harbor in August 1913 consolidating the Navy's presence in Hawai'i. The tragic sinking of an F-4 submarine off Honolulu killed the twenty-one men aboard, and was the U.S. Navy's first submarine disaster. In responding to the sinking, the worth of having a major naval shipyard in Hawai'i was shown. Shipyard workers and sailors based at Pearl Harbor raised the sub and towed it into the shipyard for a refitting. America's entry into World War I in 1918 highlighted the need for a first-class naval base at Pearl Harbor capable of taking care of the Pacific fleet in time of war. As the strategic importance of Pearl Harbor grew, its use as a commercial port was ended, quashing the plans of maritime transport companies Matson Steamship Co. and American Hawaiian Co. for its use to supplement Honolulu Harbor.

By 1919, some $20 million in federal dollars had been spent building up the Pearl Harbor base. In the 1920s, a boost in funding for Pearl Harbor and other military bases on O'ahu, made the military the fourth largest industry in Hawai'i after sugar, pineapple, and tourism. Naval shipyard payrolls, spending by sailors in port, local contractors working on base, and expanding rail lines to the bases all aided the local economy.

Navy battleships steamed to Pearl Harbor in 1925 for extensive fleet exercises, and in 1937 concrete moorings along the shore of Ford Island became Battleship Row, the home port for the huge ships around which the Pacific fleet operated.

Submarine training and repairs expanded at a facility separate from the main base. A 134-foot submarine escape training tank became a landmark, its striped international orange and white tower erected in 1932. By 1934, about $42 million had been spent on the development of Pearl Harbor.

While battleships could enter Pearl Harbor, it was no easy feat for the ship officers and crews. They had to make a tight turn after backing off on their screws to pass through the entrance to Pearl Harbor. To remedy this, Congress provided funding for further dredging at the harbor entrance and improvements and upgrades at the naval base and shipyard. Now Pearl Harbor was in the same class as Navy yards at Bremerton in Puget Sound and at Mare Island in San Francisco Bay.

The number of enlisted men based at Pearl Harbor grew from about 600 in 1925 to just over 1,000 in 1936. By 1940, some $100 million in federal funding had been invested in Pearl Harbor, and it now spread out over 10,000 acres. A row of drydocks linked by a marine railway and supported by industrial shops provided ship repairs and improvements. Warships and submarines and Navy airplanes stood sentinel for American interests at the Crossroads of the Pacific.

The commander-in-chief of the Pacific Fleet led the sea forces that covered the largest ocean in the world. In the balmy, pre–World War II territorial era, few foresaw that Pearl Harbor would soon be the place where America *began* fighting a global war. ■

WORLD WAR I NATATORIUM MEMORIAL

The historic Beaux Arts–style Waikīkī Natatorium War Memorial is dedicated to the memory of the 10,000 men and women of Hawai'i who served during World War I. Overseas they served in the Army and Navy, as Red Cross workers, and as battlefield nurses and ambulance drivers in France. In Hawai'i, local residents entertained visiting troops, purchased Liberty Loans war bonds, made bandages to send to the war, and patrolled Hawaiian waters, where a German gunboat, its tender, and a schooner were seized. Some served with British forces. The German-owned Hackfeld & Co. sugar industry conglomerate was reorganized and emerged as patriotic-named American Factors. Hawai'i troops garrisoned all the Army posts in the Islands when the regulars of the U.S. Army were sent to the war.

Roll of Honor plaque stands in front of the Waikīkī Natatorium War Memorial honoring those who served in WWI. [Gay Wong]

The Daughters and Sons of Hawaiian Warriors organization first proposed creating a memorial honoring the World War I veterans. In 1919, the Territorial Legislature approved the acquisition of a parcel between the shoreline and Kalākaua Avenue near picturesque Sans Souci beach. The dedication of the memorial site by the Hawai'i chapter of the newly formed American Legion was held on the first anniversary of the Armistice.

In 1920, a blue-ribbon committee announced plans to build an Olympic-size, 100-meter saltwater pool known as the Natatorium. Like a giant picture frame, the sea walls and concrete deck of the proposed pool would border a rectangle of salt water, employing as its bottom beach sand atop a flat coral reef. A regal Beaux Arts architectural design won the contest for San Francisco architect Lewis P. Hobart, a plan his firm saw as reflecting "the highly individual color and flavor of Hawaii and Honolulu."

In combining a war memorial with a sports arena, Hobart sought to create a memorable and functional open-air swimming arena. As an inspiration, Hobart drew upon the reflecting pool fronting the Lincoln Memorial in Washington, D.C. He also ensured that the pool would be functional, building it to specifications necessary in staging championship international swim meets.

The $250,000 project included the pool plus a twin set of permanent tiered bleacher seating, offering a view of Waikīkī's colorful sunsets. A signature Beaux Arts arch entrance featuring four stately stone eagles greeted swimmers and spectators. The salt water filling the pool, which dips as deep as twenty-two feet, circulated in from and out to the Pacific. The swimming area was dredged out of a shallow reef.

The Natatorium opened on August 24, 1927, with 1912 Stockholm Olympics gold medal champion Duke Kahanamoku taking the first swim. The Duke, a legendary Waikīkī beachboy and international surfing pioneer, remarked, "I certainly had the thrill of my life—the crowd. I will never forget it. The intense interest shown by everybody, the color, that wonderful Waikiki pool, I had to rub my eyes and pinch myself to see if it were not all a dream."

The Natatorium, then the largest open-ocean swimming stadium in the world, drew national no-

Completed in 1927, the Waikīkī Natatorium War Memorial was built to remember the men and women who served during World War I. It was built in the Hawaiian Beaux-Arts architectural style. Now in disrepair, its future use is being debated. [Hawai'i State Archives]

tice when swimmers from the mainland and Japan arrived to compete against Hawai'i swimmers in the AAU National Championships. World record holder Johnny Weissmuller of California won the 100-, 400-, and 800-meter events. His triumph led to offers from Hollywood, with Weissmuller later playing Tarzan on the silver screen. Buster Crabbe won the 1500-meter event. Punahou graduate Crabbe went on to fame playing Flash Gordon in films.

Once opened, the Natatorium's seawalls provided a safe venue for swimming lessons for children away from ocean currents and waves. Lessons were provided for kids from local families and from military families stationed in Hawai'i.

After the Pearl Harbor attack on December 7, 1941, the U.S. Army closed the pool to the public and turned the Natatorium into a training facility. In 1949, postwar refurbishing of the memorial pool began and its oversight was turned over to the City and County of Honolulu. In the postwar era, its condition deteriorated, mostly due to poor water quality.

The Natatorium was permanently closed in 1979 due to its derelict condition. Since then, a controversy has grown over whether to demolish or preserve the Natatorium. Subsequent restoration work restored the bleachers and entrance, but the pool deck is now collapsing in places and the pool itself is in poor condition.

One plan is to level the Natatorium pool and move the memorial arch away from the beach closer to Kalākaua Avenue. One future use of the site could be beach volleyball courts.

The Friends of the Natatorium are lobbying to preserve and restore the Natatorium to its original condition. The memorial was listed in 1980 on the National Register of Historic Places. Proponents cite a design that would reduce in half the volume of the pool and place silica sand atop the shallow reef below the surface, along with stabilizing its ocean walls and pool deck. ■

Aircraft destroyed on the ground at Ford Island in Pearl Harbor. In the background, the smoke and flames of giant battleships destroyed at their berths. [U.S. Navy-National Archives]

THE PEARL HARBOR
ATTACK

BEFORE THE ATTACK

The 72nd Bombardment Squadron flying near Pearl Harbor on February 26, 1932. On December 7, 1941, the base at Pearl Harbor was on a minimum state of alert, with its secondary and antiaircraft guns ready to fire immediately. The total number of combat aircraft in the Islands on December 6, however, was just 221, with only 119 in commission. The other planes were being overhauled to send to the Philippines. [U.S. Army Museum of Hawai'i]

Japanese and American officials reviewing troops, Wheeler Field, 1929. [Baker-Van Dyke Collection]

The American fleet lies anchored in Pearl Harbor on May 2, 1940. On the afternoon of December 6, 1941, as the aircraft carrier USS *Enterprise* was on maneuvers at sea, the remaining ships that were the pride of the United States Navy were similarly moored along Battleship Row next to Ford Island (center). [U.S. Army Museum of Hawai'i]

THE DAY OF INFAMY

Sunday, December 7, 1941, dawned peacefully on O'ahu. The Island's civilians and military personnel arose on the sunny morning assuming it would be just another relaxing, balmy weekend day. The day would soon become one that everyone in America would remember as the Day of Infamy, a moment in time they would always recall and know where they were and what they were doing.

Few knew that at 03:42 hours an order went out to the patrol destroyer USS *Ward* to search for an unidentified submarine spotted about one mile outside the entrance to the mid-Pacific headquarters of the U.S. Navy's Pacific Fleet: Pearl Harbor.

Navy strategists had moved the Pacific Fleet from San Diego in 1940 to protect the Philippines, to serve as a sentinel for the Panama Canal, and to be closer to the Navy's remote bases to the west at Midway and Wake islands and to the southwest at Johnston and Palmyra atolls.

In port at Pearl Harbor, called by some the "Gibraltar of the Pacific," were seven battleships moored along Battleship Row on the east shore of Ford Island and one at the nearby drydock. Dotting the lochs at Pearl Harbor were eight cruisers, thirty-five destroyers, four submarines, minelayers, seaplane tenders, repair ships, and target ships, including the USS *Utah.*

Some 43,000 troops, comprised of two infantry divisions and land defense forces, were stationed in the Islands, mostly at Schofield Barracks in central O'ahu. Artillery and antiaircraft posts lined O'ahu's south shore, ready to protect Pearl Harbor from attack.

American military leaders considered Pearl Harbor to be "the best defended naval base in the world." The Hawaiian Islands, the most isolated island group in the Pacific, were seen as impregnable. East Asia was over 3,000 miles of empty ocean away. They predicted that invaders would be detected with plenty of time for a strong response.

War with Japan and its Axis partners Germany and Italy was a distinct possibility, but not yet a settled issue. In late November 1941, a Japanese diplomatic "peace" mission was in Washington, D.C., but a stalemate between the nations remained unresolved. Japan had control of sections of eastern China and wouldn't budge, while the United States adamantly continued its embargo on shipments of American oil to Japan, cutting off about 80 percent of the island nation's oil imports. President Franklin Delano Roosevelt was notified of a possible Japanese attack on the Philippines, but his intelligence reports did not predict the Hawai'i attack.

Japanese pilots receiving instructions. [National Archives]

Before the Dawn

In the predawn hours of December 7, no one in Hawai'i knew that 300 miles north of O'ahu, a carrier fleet of Imperial Japanese Navy warships was approaching at full speed. On Saturday, December 6, life went on as usual on the Navy, Marine, and Army bases, with servicemen on regular duty, civilians enjoying a sunny weekend with ball games in parks and shopping in the department stores clustered around Fort Street in downtown Honolulu.

Tora! Tora! Tora!

On the morning of December 7, 1941, there were about 100 Navy ships present in Pearl Harbor. Eight were battleships and the rest were cruisers, destroyers, and support ships.

Half of the Pacific Fleet was out to sea or moored elsewhere, including its three aircraft carriers. The *Enterprise* was 200 miles west of Pearl Harbor, the *Lexington* was 425 miles southeast of Midway, and the *Saratoga* was being overhauled in San Diego.

The Japanese task force was disappointed that the carriers were not present but decided to go ahead with the attack and target the battleships instead. At 6 a.m. they launched the first of two waves of 353 fighters and dive bombers from six of their own carriers about 230 miles north of O'ahu.

When it became clear that the attack was a surprise, the prearranged victory call, "Tora! Tora! Tora!," was transmitted by radio back to the enemy fleet. Two minutes later, the first bombs began to fall.

All of the battleships were damaged by bombs and aerial torpedoes. Five were sunk. Eleven other ships were heavily damaged, two beyond repair. A total of 188 planes were also destroyed on the ground and another 159 damaged. The Japanese lost only twenty-nine aircraft.

In time, however, the crippled Pearl Harbor fleet came back to life. The USS *Arizona* and the USS *Utah* were the only complete losses among the battleships. The USS *California*, USS *Nevada*, and USS *Virginia* were raised, modernized, and returned to service.

The twenty Japanese ships that had participated in the Pearl Harbor air raid were all lost during the war.

A table-top mock-up of Ford Island and Pearl Harbor constructed by Japanese war planners to help stage the attack of December 7, 1941. [Hawai'i State Archives]

The Japanese Imperial Navy carrier group sailed from Yokosuka naval base in Japan on November 26, consisting of six fleet aircraft carriers, two battleships, two heavy cruisers, one light cruiser, and nine destroyers. As the warships moved in after almost two weeks at sea having sailed thousands of miles undetected, music from Honolulu radio stations was heard aboard ship.

The Japanese strategy was to stun the United States by attacking O'ahu from the air, with hopes of gaining a six-month buffer in which to deploy a north-to-south island defense in the Western Pacific—the length of time estimated to place Japanese troops and ships on a line of Pacific Islands where they would shore up defenses capable of stopping any American advance towards Japan and its "Asian Prosperity Zone" in East Asia.

The First Wave

By 6 a.m., two Japanese reconnaissance planes returned from a flight over O'ahu, radioing that the U.S. fleet was moored at Pearl Harbor and all was quiet. The carriers began to turn into the wind as pilots and flight crews prepared for their mission.

At 6:10 a.m., Vice-Admiral Chuichi Nagumo ordered a first wave of 185 planes to launch from the carriers. Mitsubishi Zero-Sen fighters took off first, approaching from the northwest shores of O'ahu, followed by high-level Nakajima "Kate" bombers and Aichi "Val"

A Japanese B5N2 level bomber over Pearl Harbor on the morning of December 7, 1941. [U.S. Army Museum of Hawai'i]

torpedo dive bombers. Within fifteen minutes the flight was in the air, with Commander Mitsuo Fuchida in the lead plane.

The destroyer *Ward* opened fire on the minisub at 6:45 a.m., hitting the sub and moving in to drop depth charges. The shots were the first fired by the United States in what would become known as the Pacific War.

At 7:02 a.m., a North Shore Army radar operator near Kahuku detected the Japanese Navy squadrons heading in from the northwest. The signal was misidentified as either a flight of new U.S. B-17 bombers heading to O'ahu from California or a flight of American carrier-based planes.

At 7:53 a.m., "Tora! Tora! Tora!" (Tiger! Tiger! Tiger!) was the coded message Commander Fuchida sent out, confirming that the ships at Pearl Harbor and Island ground forces had been completely caught by surprise and the attack was to begin.

Attacking planes flew over the Kolekole Pass, from Wai'anae to central O'ahu, west to southeast, heading straight towards Pearl Harbor, which was then in full view before them. No antiaircraft gun crews were at their stations, nor were fighter planes in the air to challenge them.

The full force of the bombing of O'ahu began at 7:55 a.m. at the Marine's Kāne'ohe Naval Air Station on the windward side. Patrol planes were lined up in tight rows to defend against on-island sabotage, making easy targets. Zero pilots would destroy every plane.

At about 7:58 a.m., minutes before the main attack on Pearl Harbor

began, a Japanese pilot jumped the gun, flying in low overhead and dropping bombs on the Ford Island Naval Air Station, where 100 aircraft were parked. A dispatch from the command center there exclaimed, "AIR RAID PEARL HARBOR THIS IS NO DRILL."

Forty Japanese bombers swept in above Pearl Harbor as blue skies emerged from the soft dawn light. Their pilots saw the rising Hawaiian sun as a good omen for the success of the attack. Sailors and Marines aboard the battleship USS *Arizona* and adjoining ships were raising flags for the daily 8 a.m. call to colors. Torpedoes dropped from low-flying fighters, churning up white foamy wakes in the inner har-

1. **Taking off from the aircraft carrier *Akagi* in the early hours of December 7, 1941, an AGMZ AI-101 Japanese fighter begins its deadly mission to Pearl Harbor. [U.S. Army Museum of Hawai'i]**

2. **Japanese Navy photo taken from attacking airplane of smoking Navy ships anchored end to end in Pearl Harbor. The USS *Oklahoma* is pictured in the top row, far right alongside the USS *Maryland.* [Hawai'i State Archives]**

bor, exploding when they struck ships. The first wave brought mayhem to the Pacific Fleet. Few antiaircraft guns were manned or even loaded. Battleships lacked anti-torpedo nets. Many sailors were incredulous; their first instinct was casting blame for the bombing on American pilots screwing up. But quickly, the servicemen made out the bright red sun "meatball" insignias on the wings of the planes, and survivors dashed to battle stations.

The air attack was like a swarm of giant hornets hovering over Pearl Harbor. Fast-turning Zeroes dropped 132-pound bombs and strafed with machine guns and cannons. A first wave of fifty-one Val dive bombers struck the air station at Ford Island, nearby Hickam Army Air Force Field, and Wheeler Field in central O'ahu. At Wheeler, hundreds of servicemen were killed in their barracks. Japanese pilots flew low enough to be shot down by troops firing rifles. Some landed aboard their carriers with telephone wires trailing from their landing gear.

Kate bombers flew in low over Battleship Row, dropping 800-kilo torpedoes radically modified to avoid diving deep in the shallow, forty-foot-draft harbor. The Japanese Navy focused their arms development on cutting-edge torpedo technology, as the island nation had been limited by World War I treaties in constructing warships.

The first ten minutes of the attack brought the most devastating damage of the day to the ships at Pearl Harbor. Bombs or torpedoes struck all eight battleships.

The USS *Arizona* exploded in a sky-high fireball, shearing her bow when a delayed-fuse, armor-piercing Japanese bomb tore its way down several decks near her No. 2 turret. A forward magazine detonated, blowing up the two million pounds of gunpowder in its hold. The USS *Arizona* fireball was a blast equivalent to 500 tons of TNT, equal to the force of a small nuclear bomb, lifting the bow of the massive battleship, thick metal plates and beams twisting akimbo. The entire USS *Arizona* brass band died. Photos and film clips of the USS *Arizona* explosion became iconic images of the Day of Infamy, rallying enlistment by millions of men and women and support for entering World War II on the home front. Half of the deaths at Pearl Harbor occurred

1. The *Akagi* was the Japanese flagship of the Pearl Harbor attack force. [U.S. Army Museum of Hawai'i]

2. Three attacks on Hickam Airfield that lasted ten minutes each left hundreds of American servicemen dead and destroyed planes on the ground, lined up with only ten feet between their wingtips. Hangars and machine shops were also badly damaged, and aircraft did not get into the air until the afternoon. Fortunately, Hickam had the longest runway in the Islands and it was unharmed. [U.S. Army Museum of Hawai'i]

1
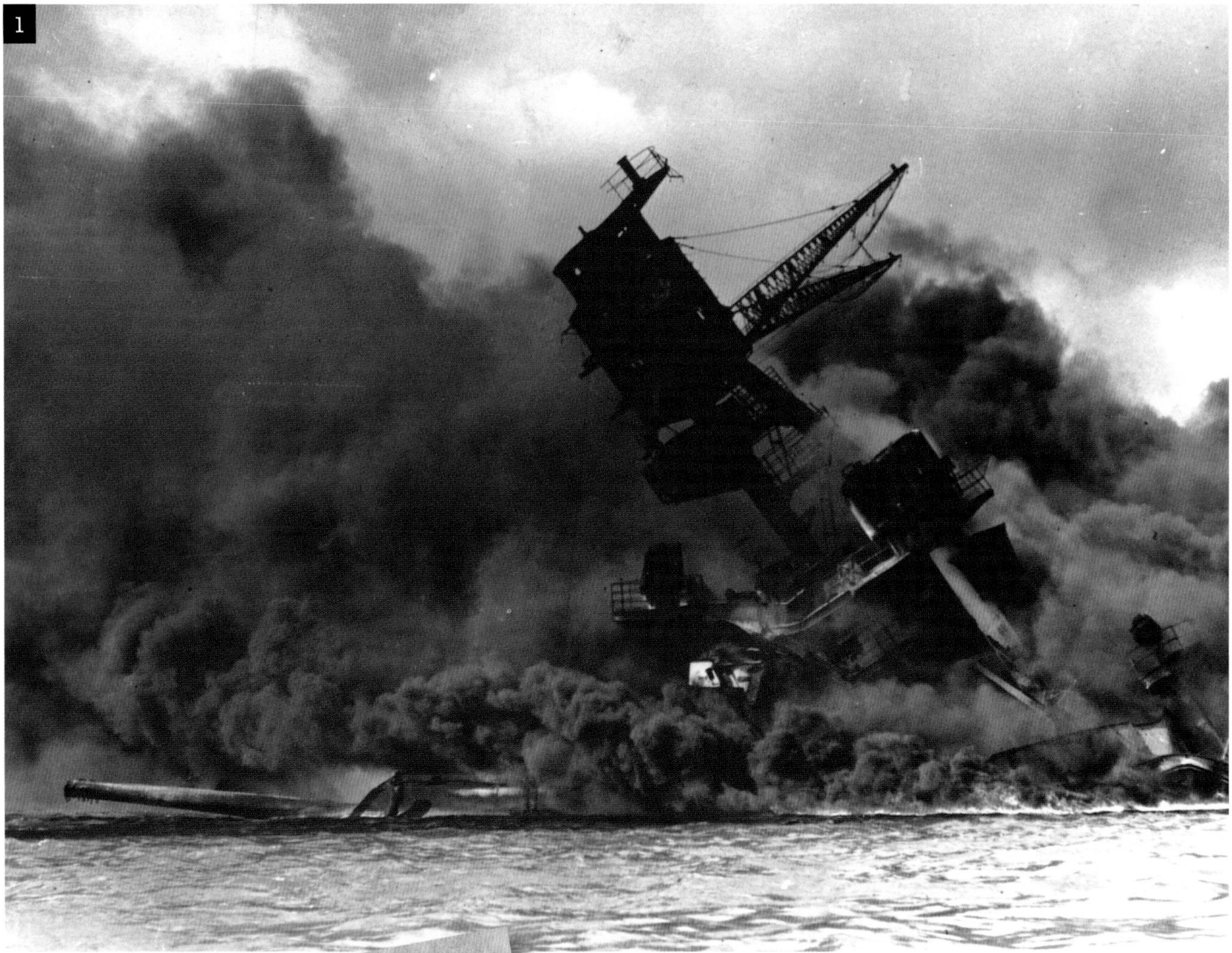

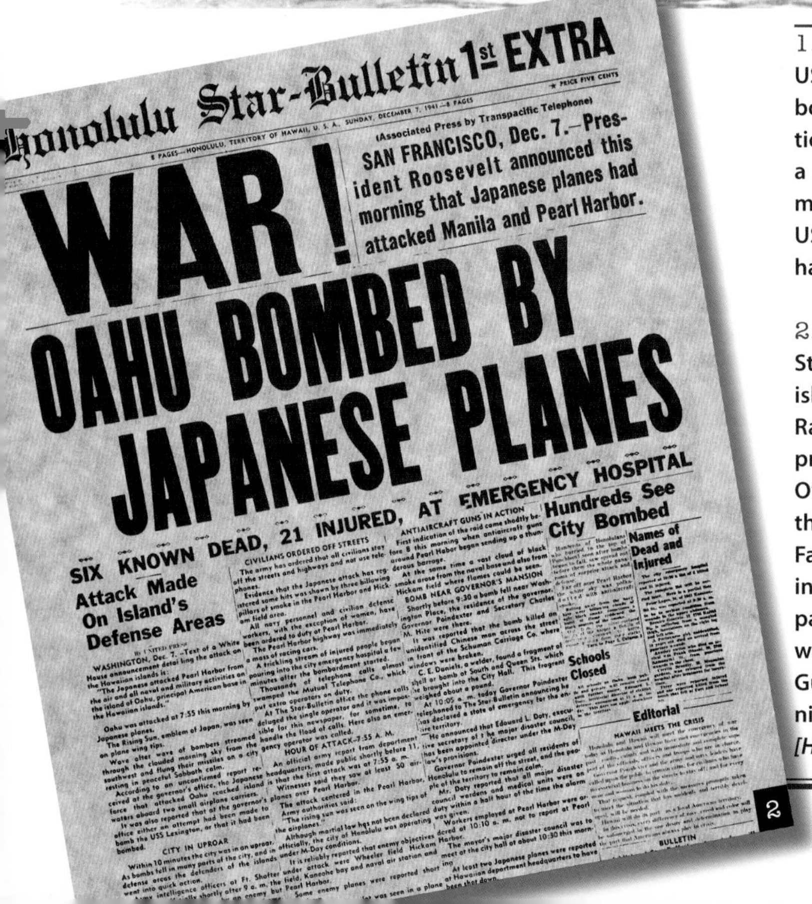
Honolulu Star-Bulletin 1st EXTRA

8 PAGES—HONOLULU, TERRITORY OF HAWAII, U.S.A., SUNDAY, DECEMBER 7, 1941—8 PAGES

PRICE FIVE CENTS

(Associated Press by Transpacific Telephone)

SAN FRANCISCO, Dec. 7.—President Roosevelt announced this morning that Japanese planes had attacked Manila and Pearl Harbor.

WAR!

OAHU BOMBED BY JAPANESE PLANES

SIX KNOWN DEAD, 21 INJURED, AT EMERGENCY HOSPITAL

Attack Made On Island's Defense Areas

Hundreds See City Bombed

Names of Dead and Injured

Schools Closed

Editorial

2

1. During the first few minutes of the Pearl Harbor attack, the USS *Arizona* took a hit from a 1,760-pound armor-piercing bomb that slammed through the deck. The forward ammunition magazine instantly exploded with a horrific blast that sent a column of black smoke spiraling from the ship. Within nine minutes, as burning oil turned the ocean into an inferno, the USS *Arizona* and 1,177 of her crew sank to the bottom of the harbor. [National Archives]

2. The frightening headline and front page of the Honolulu Star-Bulletin offered the only news available that afternoon to islanders eager to know details of the attack on Pearl Harbor. Radio transmissions at commercial stations were shut down to prevent the enemy from using the signals as a beacon to locate O'ahu. On the evening of December 7, 1941, residents braced themselves for what they believed would be another attack. False rumors spread through Honolulu that the water supply in Makiki had been poisoned by saboteurs, and that Japanese parachutists were seen landing in the valleys. Barbed wire was spread across the beaches at Waikīkī as nervous National Guardsmen fingered the triggers of their rifles through the night, waiting for the invasion which would never take place. *[Honolulu Star-Bulletin].*

1

U. S. S. RANGER

NAVAL DISPATCH

Heading: NSS NR 977 Z ØF8 1830 ØF3 ØF4 0 BT

AIR RAID ON PEARL HARBOR X THIS IS NOT DRILL

EXECUTIVE

Date 7 DEC 41 ED

From: CINCPAC

To: CINCLANT COMAF OPNAV

Info:

ACTION

INFO

2

on the USS *Arizona,* with 1,177 men dying aboard, including her admiral and captain. Fires spread across the hulk of the ship.

The target ship USS *Utah,* moored on the west shore of Ford Island, capsized at 8:10 a.m. The battleships USS *Oklahoma* and fleet flagship USS *California* were heavily damaged. The USS *Nevada* survived, attempting to power out to sea but wary of blocking the narrow entrance to Pearl Harbor, a channel only 374 yards wide and 3,500 yards long.

The command network of the Pacific Fleet and its air support on O'ahu were shattered. Individual ships and bases were on their own in defending against the Japanese attack. Surviving men and women of Pearl Harbor responded heroically, taking action at guns and in rescue efforts. Hundreds of men were trapped in the hulls of sunken ships, many entombed forever.

Fortunately, not all the Pacific Fleet was moored at Pearl Harbor. An equal number of ships were at sea or anchored at San Diego and other ports. The Hawai'i-based aircraft carrier USS *Saratoga* was in for repairs at San Diego; the carrier USS *Lexington* was off the Northwestern Hawaiian Islands; and the carrier USS *Enterprise* was out on maneuvers west of Kaua'i.

3

1. Naval dispatch from the Commander in Chief Pacific announcing the Japanese attack on Pearl Harbor. [Library of Congress]

2: This photograph, taken during the attack on Pearl Harbor, shows Japanese aircraft still above the base before returning to their carriers. Japan lost less than a hundred men and only twenty-nine aircraft. [U.S. Army Museum of Hawai'i]

3. The Pearl Harbor attack in progress. [U.S. Army Museum of Hawai'i]

1. Billowing smoke rising from explosions at the Pearl Harbor attack are seen from 'Aiea. [Baker-Van Dyke Collection]

2. The Japanese air attack on Pearl Harbor on December 7, 1941, plunged the United States into World War II. [U.S. Navy]

3. Battleship row following the attack on Pearl Harbor. [U.S. Navy/University of Hawai'i War Records Depository]

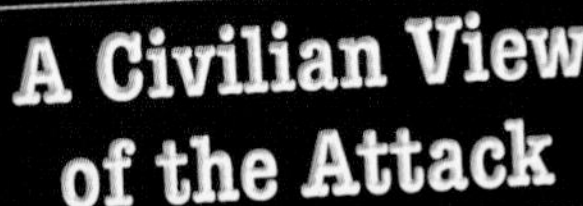

A Civilian View of the Attack

People were standing in front of their stores or homes as if in a state of shock. When I passed by Bertania and Richards Street, I remember seeing the blood of a civilian splattered on the sidewalk. He had died when a bomb landed across the street on Governor Poindexter's driveway at Washingon Place. At Queen's Hospital, the many bodies of the dead were laid out on the lawn because there wasn't enough space in the hospital.

—A resident of Honolulu, Oral History, 1941.

The Second Wave

The first wave of attack planes began to return to the Japanese carriers at about 8:30 a.m., now 190 miles north of O'ahu. A second wave was launched at 8:50 a.m., ordered this time to attack O'ahu from the northeast. Fifty-four Val bombers targeted Hickam Field, and eighty-one dive bombers attacked the drydocks at Pearl Harbor. A coat of thick oil covered Pearl Harbor waters, and uninjured men, some from the shipyard, dived in to rescue injured sailors and Marines.

The second-wave pilots faced opposition not there when the first wave screamed in from Kolekole Pass. Pillars of smoke climbed into the mid-Sunday morning sky, providing cover for Pearl Harbor, and the attack planes now passed through banks of antiaircraft fire. Pilots flying P-38 fighters took off from Hale'iwa Field on the North Shore, an airfield remaining open during the attack, and engaged the Zeroes above Wheeler Field. To avoid blocking the entrance channel to Pearl Harbor, at 9:10 a.m. the captain of the *Nevada* battleship ran her aground at Hospital Point.

The assault ended two hours later. Twenty-one ships were sunk or damaged. Over 300 American aircraft were destroyed or damaged. Some 2,403 military personnel, over 1,000 from the USS *Arizona*, and 57 civilians were dead. Japanese losses were comparatively light—fewer than thirty planes downed.

1. The attack on Pearl Harbor was so unexpected that at first many civilians reacted with curiosity, believing the aerial bombardment was simply a very realistic military exercise. Above the harbor at Halawa Heights, hundreds gawked at the destruction as a radio broadcaster warned Honolulu residents that the attack was" the real McCoy." This group stood nonchalantly on a city street corner in the early stage of the assault, unaware of the dangers they faced. Mistimed antiaircraft shells fell back on Honolulu with terrible consequences, and dozens of homes and buildings were destroyed, 300 civilians injured, and 57 men, women, and children killed. [National Archives]

2. Damage at King and McCully Streets, December 7, 1941. [Hawai'i War Records Depository/University of Hawai'i at Mānoa]

At 11 a.m., Commander Fuchida surveyed the damage at Pearl Harbor from the air. Satisfied, he turned north to fly back to his aircraft carrier.

On the ground, O'ahu's people were shocked. Improperly armed antiaircraft shells exploded on the ground rather than in the air, destroying homes in Honolulu and killing civilians. Japanese fighters strafed automobiles on country roads and shot up the Waialua Sugar Mill. False reports spread like wildfire, claiming Japanese troops were landing on beaches.

Order began to return by the afternoon. The Japanese embassy in Honolulu was raided. The Army ordered a blackout to begin at sundown. Governor Poindexter declared martial law.

The Third Wave

At 1 p.m., Fuchida landed on board the carrier *Akagi* and discussed launching a third wave attack.

Though the American forces were caught completely by surprise, the attack could have been vastly more devastating. Despite the two bombing runs by Imperial Japanese Navy planes crippling the American fleet at Pearl Harbor, support facilities at Pearl Harbor escaped relatively undamaged. The Japanese attackers failed to destroy the Pearl Harbor Naval Shipyard and its drydocks or the above-ground oil storage tank farms that held the Pacific Fleet fuel supply at Pearl Harbor. Many damaged ships were repaired quickly, ready to fight another day, and there was no need to rebuild the fuel tanks nor to wait for a months-long resupply of fuel from the mainland, which could have left the Hawaiian Islands wide open to a Japanese invasion.

By the end of the day, Pearl Harbor, little known outside of Hawai'i, was on center stage in the world news, and America was on the threshold of entering the greatest armed conflict in history, awaiting a declaration of war by President Roosevelt and Congress.

About two dozen cables stretched out from the naval shipyard at Pearl Harbor, as seen from the air, are connected to a battleship sunk on December 7, 1941 along Ford Island. In the months following the attack, shipyard workers welded patches over bomb holes to seal the sunken hulls and then attached the long cables to roll the ships to an upright position for repairs or salvage. [Hawai'i State Archives]

On August 10, 1944, Admiral Nimitz points to the Japanese home islands on a large map of the Western Pacific to an audience of General Douglas MacArthur, President Franklin D. Roosevelt and Admiral William Healy. Nimitz argued strenuously with maps and intelligence information that fighting the Japanese in the Philippines would be unnecessary. By neutralizing Japan's airbases in the region, the U.S. Navy could instead go on to invade Formosa and launch an attack on Japan. General MacArthur then rose and, speaking without maps or notes, told President Roosevelt that bypassing the Philippines would be politically and militarily disastrous. "American public opinion will condemn you," he finally stated. "And it will be justified." With a re-election campaign only months away, FDR approved MacArthur's highly publicized "return to the Philippines." [Hawai'i War Records Depository/University of Hawai'i at Mānoa]

The Pearl Harbor attack ranks as a major event in U.S. history as well as in Hawaiian history. Questions lingered for decades, and still do, as to why American forces were seemingly totally unprepared, even though war with Japan seemed imminent.

Operation Z

"Operation Hawaii" (or Operation Z) was the code name given by Admiral Isoroku Yamamoto for the attack on the Hawaiian Islands. The initial phase was planned as an aerial strike on U.S. air and naval forces on the Island of O'ahu. This was to be followed within hours by additional bombardment of the drydocks, supply depots, and oil reserves at Pearl Harbor. Not only would the American military be crippled, but their ability to repair the damage would be seriously hampered. Finally, "Operation Hawaii" was to include a massive land invasion weeks later by the Japanese Imperial Army on O'ahu's North Shore. The belief was that the United States would rather negotiate for peace than spill more blood in the distant Hawaiian Islands. Thus Japan could successfully seize Hawai'i as the eastern boundary of their Pacific defense system. Because the USS *Enterprise* was not at Pearl Harbor during the first attack, Admiral Chuichi Nagumo, commander of the strike force, decided that a second attack on the drydocks would be too risky. Full implementation of "Operation Hawaii" was therefore aborted, and the attack fleet returned to Japan.

With construction areas and supply depots undamaged, the U.S. Navy began a massive repair of its fleet, which six months later defeated Japanese naval forces at Midway Island. ■

Preparation for a Japanese invasion involved stringing miles of barbed wire and camouflaging buildings along the coastlines of all the Islands. Waikīkī Beach was outfitted for war by 1,200 civilian volunteers, the "Kiawe Corps," working in early 1942. The task of re-painting large buildings like the pineapple cannery, the electric generator plant and Aloha Tower was left to the Army Corps of Engineers. Camouflage nets were also needed to cover gun emplacements and air raid warning systems. To construct them, motion picture and stage designers were brought in and former lei-sellers wove scraps of burlap into nets about twenty feet square. Even flowers were used to hide some military installations, and Punahou School's football field was disguised by planting a quarter of a million seedlings. [Hawai'i State Archives]

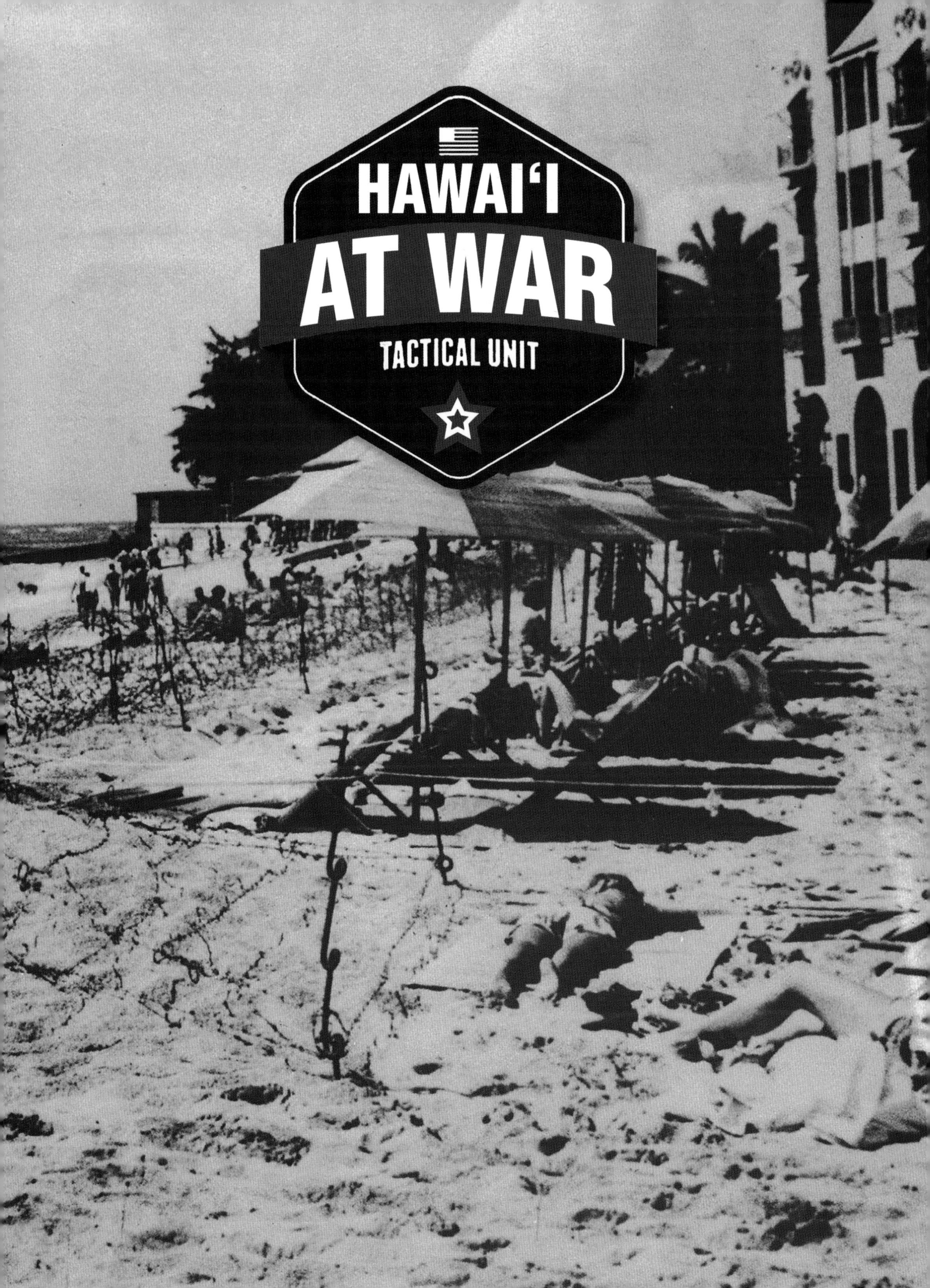
HAWAI‘I
AT WAR
TACTICAL UNIT

1. In the first months of the war, gas masks were mandatory for all civilians. This photograph of men, women and children waiting in line for them at Farrington High School was taken in January of 1942. Under martial law, civilians not properly equipped were subject to fines. Many restaurants added a "gas-mask check" to the usual "hat and coat check" service to accommodate their patrons. [National Archives]

2. Roosevelt High School students cut material for rebuilding children's gas masks, May 18, 1942. *[Honlulu Star-Bulletin/*University of Hawai'i War Records Depository/HWRD0382]

"KGBQ to car 20," called the calm voice of Honolulu police dispatcher Jimmy Wong one Sunday morning. "Complainant reported a bomb fell through his house while he was having breakfast." Several minutes later, another message went out: "KGBQ to car 30. An unknown woman reported a bomb fell near Lewers and Kalakaua." Soon many more frantic phone calls from all over the city poured into the police switchboard. As various patrol units responded to a variety of disturbances, the magnitude of what was taking place assumed unbelievable proportions. Dispatcher Wong finally called out to all police cars and radio stations that planes were bombing Pearl Harbor. Everything was on fire.

"This is the real McCoy, " radio announcer Webley Edwards shouted into his microphone at the KGMB station later on the morning of December 7, 1941. "O'ahu is under air attack. " Hundreds of civilians ran outside to watch and quickly realized that the billowing smoke and exploding gas tanks were not mock military maneuvers. Squadrons of Japanese dive-bombers and Mitsubishi Zeroes swarmed over Diamond Head. Shock and confusion turned to chaos as the damage spread and death tolls mounted. Dozens of civilians died, in

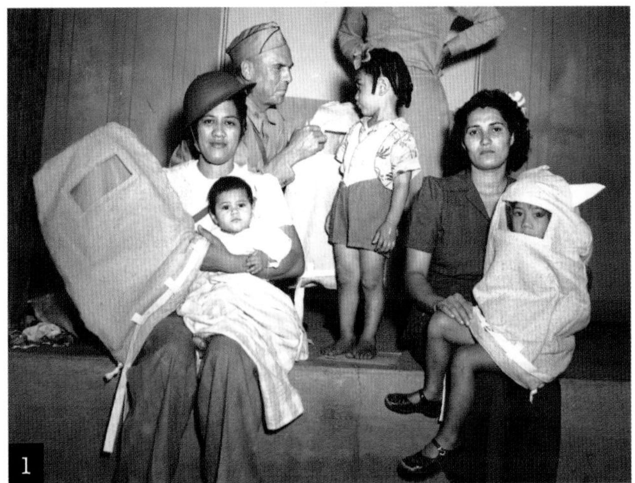

addition to more than 2,300 military personnel, including the doomed servicemen of the USS *Arizona.*

After a phone consultation with President Franklin Roosevelt, the governor of Hawai'i declared martial law. Military authorities assumed control of territorial courts and law enforcement agencies. All saloons were closed and a sunset curfew and total blackout were made compulsory.

Within days, the Islands were braced for a Japanese invasion. Armed sentries stood guard at public utilities, and sandbagged machine-gun nests looked down on city streets. For the first time, major thoroughfares were made one way to accommodate emergency vehicles and masses of khaki-colored jeeps, trucks, and tanks. Familiar landmarks such as Aloha Tower were painted in camouflage to conceal them from air attack. Civil Defense workers, ROTC units, and the Territorial Guard stretched barbed wire across beaches. Over 20,000 civilian volunteers eventually bolstered the military.

At night, no lights could show from a business or residence, and special bulbs and window coverings were required for homes. All cars had to have blacked-out headlights, and very few could drive at night during curfew. Civilians were issued thousands of gas masks, with full-body "bunny masks" for infants. "Scare pukas," or bomb shelters, were dug throughout the Islands, with 250 on

1. Col. George F. Unmacht, department chemical officer, prepares to fit a "bunny" gas mask on a skeptical child at Pohukaina school. On the left are Mrs. Elizabeth I, Jr. and Barbara Jean Akau, and on the right, Mrs. Doris Akau and Edith Mau, June 6, 1942. *[Honolulu Star-Bulletin/*University of Hawai'i War Records Depository/HWRD0384]

2: Edean Ross of the Military Governor's Office peeks out of an air raid shelter (covered type) in downtown Honolulu, 1942. *[Honolulu Star-Bulletin/*University of Hawai'i War Records Depository/HWRD0101]

3: An air raid shelter (covered type) on Central Intermediate School grounds, 1942. *[Honolulu Star-Bulletin/*University of Hawai'i War Records Depository/HWRD0102]

1. World War II affected every aspect of civilian life. From food control and gasoline rationing to "victory gardens," bomb shelters, gas masks, and sales of war bonds, the need to organize the war effort was emphasized by posters displayed throughout the Islands. [University of Hawai'i War Records Depository]

2. Three young scouts salvage old rubber from a service station located at Bertania St. (in back), 1942. [*Honolulu Star-Bulletin*/University of Hawai'i War Records Depository/HWRD0645]

3. Students from Kapalama school worked to collect aluminum for U.S. airplanes as their contribution to the city's aluminum drive. [*Honolulu Star-Bulletin*/University of Hawai'i War Records Depository/HWRD0650]

4. Floyd W. Fitzpatrick, secretary-manager of the Honolulu Junior Chamber of Commerce, presents a $400 check to the USO. Receiving it are, left to right, Gunda Reid, Florence Thompson, Jackie Tatum and Alyce Louis, members of the USO Camp Shows group. The money was raised through the junior chamber's Salvage for Victory campaign. [*Honolulu Star-Bulletin*/University of Hawai'i War Records Depository/HWRD0641]

O'ahu meant to provide for 70,000 people. Every citizen of Hawai'i had to be fingerprinted, the first such mass identification effort in the history of the United States.

Recognizing that the invading Japanese Army would seize any available cash, the government ordered civilians to turn in all their U.S. currency. More than $200 million was burned at a crematorium and a sugar mill, and new bills were issued with a "HAWAII" imprint, making them useless to invaders.

Beaches, gasoline storage tanks, military bases, and Honolulu Harbor were declared restricted areas. Civilian populations were immediately evacuated.

Property owned by Japanese aliens—banks, department stores, language schools, and Shinto shrines—were confiscated by the military. Authorities also occupied private and public property for hospital use or as military housing and offices. The presence of the American armed forces was felt from Punahou School to 'Iolani Palace to the Royal Hawaiian Hotel.

Within forty-eight hours of the attack on Pearl Harbor, hundreds of Japanese, German, and Italian aliens

1. **A Civilian Defense Air Raid Test during which downtown Honolulu was evacuated. A crowd forms on the bridge on River Street just outside the evacuation area. Gas bombs can be seen below the bridge. [U.S. Army Signal Corps/University of Hawai'i War Records Depository/HWRD1169]**

2. **A group of children being taken by their teachers to an area outside the business district during an air raid alert evacuation. *[Honolulu Star-Bulletin/*University of Hawai'i War Records Depository/HWRD0511]**

1. Recreation for enlisted men at the Royal Hawaiian Hotel, April 8, 1942. *[Honolulu Star-Bulletin/*University of Hawai'i War Records Depository/ HWRD0626]

2. U.S. Engineer office in a school room on Punahou Campus, 1940. *[Honolulu Star-Bulletin/*University of Hawai'i War Records Depository/HWRD0868]

3. The Kaimuki Victory Garden dedication. Some of the guests at the program, left to right: Mrs. G.W. Sumner, president of the Garden club; Mrs. Grace B. Wilder, executive secretary of the Outdoor circle; Col W.R. White, director of the office of food control; Mrs. E.E. Black, president of the Outdoor circle; Col. Thomas H. Green, executive in the Military Governor's Office, and Mayor Petrie. At extreme right is Riley H. Allen, editor of *The Star-Bulletin* and chairman of the program. *[Honolulu Star-Bulletin/*University of Hawai'i War Records Depository/HWRD0787]

4. Mr. Johnson and Mr. Sousa at the office of the Kaimuki Victory Garden, May 6, 1942. [Hawai'i War Research Depository]

were arrested by military intelligence officers and the FBI. A total of 1,875 resident Japanese were held by the U.S. government during the war and sent to relocation centers or internment camps on the mainland. While the majority of Japanese in Hawai'i were left relatively undisturbed by military authorities, all weapons, shortwave radios, and cameras were confiscated. The once-familiar kimono disappeared from city streets, as did the Japanese language. "Speak American" posters and campaigns equated language with patriotism, and the older alien community increasingly relied on their American-born children during this troubled, frightening time. Military regulations not only invaded the personal lives of civilians but radicalized the cultural climate.

The war effort brought hundreds of thousands of new Caucasian faces to the Islands; an estimated one million GIs passed through between 1941 and 1945. City buses were soon jam-packed with Army and Navy personnel on leave. Bars, honky-tonks, barbershops, movie houses, tattoo parlors, and the River Street brothels thrived. A confiscated Japanese department store was transformed into the USO Victory Club, one of Honolulu's best and largest social centers. Forty thousand men and women from the Islands served in the armed forces, thousands of Japanese American men enlisted in the famed 100th "Purple Heart" Battalion and 442nd Combat Regiment, which became the most-decorated unit in U.S. military history.

On August 15, 1945, the people of Hawai'i learned that World War II had come to a victorious end. The city went wild. For four years citizens had lived under martial law, military restrictions, censorship, and suspicion—all now things of the past. Yet it quickly became clear that their familiar Island home had been forever altered. The idyllic calm of the "sugar-coated fortress" was shattered, as a new population of working-class Caucasians settled in Hawai'i. These new haoles were not part of a ruling elite but rubbed shoulders with local mechanics, ditch-diggers, waitresses, etc. ■

1. A part of the Victory Club lobby in the building at King and Bethel Streets. *[Honolulu Star-Bulletin/*University of Hawai'i War Records Depository/HWRD721]

2. Pacific jubilee program at USO Victory Club honored African-American servicemen. Pictured around a wooden wagon made by Lloyd Resure, USN are four admiring servicemem. *[Honolulu Star-Bulletin/*University of Hawai'i War Records Depository/HWRD0769]

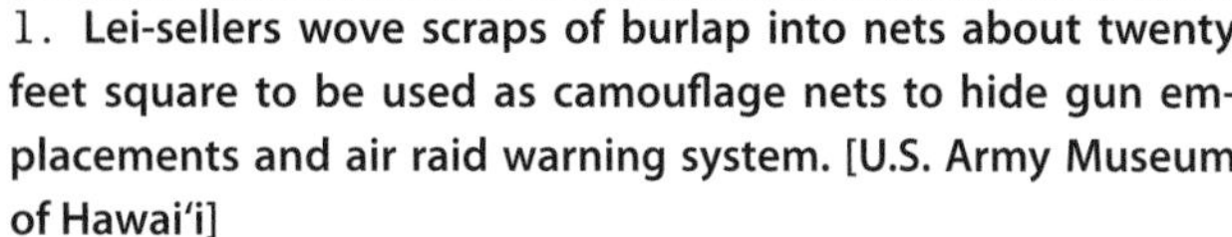

1. Lei-sellers wove scraps of burlap into nets about twenty feet square to be used as camouflage nets to hide gun emplacements and air raid warning system. [U.S. Army Museum of Hawai'i]

2. The dyeing of fabric at a camouflage factory in Honolulu, July 27, 1943. [U.S. Army Signal Corps/University of Hawai'i War Records Depository/HWRD1185]

3. At USO Victory Club, Stanley Kazmierski, a Marine, gets a lei and a kiss from Miss June Kilbey, Honolulu USO volunteer. [*Honolulu Star-Bulletin*/University of Hawai'i War Records Depository/HWRD0708]

4. Civilians cooperated with the Army and Navy in a December 7, 1943 bond drive. Posing in one of the fifteen special booths are, (left to right), Sergeant Lawrence C. George, Pittsfield, Mass., Mrs. Lois Cartwright, secretary at the USO Army & Navy YMCA, and Paul Kalamen, electricians mate first class of Grant City, Staten Island, N.Y. [*Honolulu Star-Bulletin*/University of Hawai'i War Records Depository/HWRD0222]

In January of 1943, when Japanese Americans were allowed to volunteer for the Army, their initial response was an enthusiastic rush to induction centers. Over forty percent of Nisei men between the ages of eighteen and thirty-five enlisted. Their motives were diverse. Many were patriots eager to serve the war effort, or wanted to have the opportunity to leave Hawai'i and see the world. More than a few volunteered because their friends had and they didn't want to be left out. Yet, whatever their initial reasons, as the war progressed, they became aware that their performance was being watched by the nation and was considered a test of loyalty to the land of their birth.

1. After taking their oath of service, 2. young Nisei men lined up at Schofield Barracks to receive their serial numbers. [Hawai'i State Archives; U.S. Army Museum of Hawai'i]

3, 4. "Loose Lips Sink Ships" was a constant fear for Hawai'i's military government, which attempted to minimize the flow of sensitive information into the civilian population. All letters handled by the U.S. Post Office were censored for any mention of ship movements, and indecipherable words were cut out. To encourage the entire population to "Serve in Silence, " in 1944 a parade was conducted on downtown Hotel Street. Store display windows were decorated with posters and slogans to remind everyone that "Rumors Delay Victory." [U. S. Army Museum of Hawai'i]

CAMP TARAWA

Martial law imposed following the attack on Pearl Harbor silenced the life rhythms of Hawai'i Island's sleepy sugar plantations, which until then had been punctuated by the whistle of the mills.

It was thought that with its poorly defended isolation, Hawai'i Island would be a sure target for a follow-up attack. There was a threat that the Island could become a staging area for invasion of the rest of Hawai'i. To deter an invasion, the American military police stormed into little towns, enforcing nightly blackouts, appropriating radios and pickup trucks. To defend the rugged shores of the Island, the military constructed machine-gun nests and unrolled miles of barbed wire.

Nerves were taut. Three weeks after Pearl Harbor, a lone Japanese submarine fired at some oil storage tanks on the shore at Hilo. Although it appeared to be an isolated incident, the attack fueled islanders' fears. Distrust grew. About a hundred Japanese residents on Hawai'i Island were sent to internment camps on O'ahu and the mainland.

The key sugar port of Māhukona on the Kohala Coast closed. Farmers and ranchers were directed to drive stakes into their lands to prevent the enemy from landing in planes.

Men, women, and children toted around heavy gas masks. Rationing came for purchases of liquor, rice, gasoline, and tires. Hundreds of islanders were drafted or volunteered to fight in the war. To ensure a steady food supply, residents planted victory gardens with seeds provided by the government. Those farmers who were not drafted planted more crops to supply the Army's food center in Hilo. Communities organized their own volunteer militia battalions of Hawai'i Rifles. Mothers whose own sons had left for the war cared for American soldiers stationed and training on Hawai'i Island. Of-

Thousands of Marines training to do battle in the South Pacific bunked in large field tents set up on the edge of rainy Waimea in the foothills of the Kohala Mountains. [Pacific War Memorial Assocation]

1. The flag flies at half mast at a Fifth Marine Division cemetery. Some Marines from the Fifth Division who trained at Camp Tarawa went into combat for the first time in 1945 at the bloody Battle of Iwo Jima. The Fifth suffered the largest number of casualties in the invasion of the volcanic island located within air bombing range of the Japanese mainland. [Pacific War Memorial Assocation]

2. A Fifth Marine band performs with a backdrop of the Kohala Mountains. [Pacific War Memorial Assocation]

3. The Fifth Marine Division marches in Waimea Park. A horse-mounted company trails the marching Marines, perhaps made up of local men formed into volunteer units.[Pacific War Memorial Assocation]

1. The cavalry battalion ends the daily parade at Waimea Ball Park. Circa 1940s. [Pacific War Memorial Association]
2. The 2nd Division mascot. [Pacific War Memorial Assocation]
3. The Marine Band parades through town, possibly Main Street in Honoka'a. 1945. [Pacific War Memorial Assocation]
4. Kama Rock, the theatre inside Camp Tarawa. [Pacific War Memorial Assocation]

fering a sense of home, they did laundry, cooked meals, and heated bathwater for the Marines.

Despite the war, sugar production across the Island continued as before, thanks to local women replacing the men in the plantation fields. Schools closed earlier in the afternoon, freeing students to help in the fields. U.S. Army men, posted to guard Hawai'i Island against invasion by Japanese forces, departed following the decisive U.S. Navy victory against a Japanese carrier fleet in the Battle of Midway in the spring of 1942. Military strategists decided that the threat to the Island had dissipated.

In December 1943, Marines of the Second Division, back from the bloody battle of Tarawa, arrived in the upcountry ranch town of Waimea to set up camp. The Second Division had played a major role in the victorious invasion of Tarawa Atoll in the central Pacific's Gilbert islands. The Marines, pitching their tents on Parker Ranch land outside of Waimea town, had survived one of the bloodiest battles in military history. The battle-weary soldiers arrived ready for rest and recuperation. They were exhausted, feverish from malaria and other jungle infections, and traumatized.

The Marines arrived on Island with nothing but the torn clothes on their backs. After a rough journey from Hilo, their ride from Waimea town to Parker Ranch broke down, forcing them to walk for miles to reach their temporary accommodations. The makeshift camp

lacked the basics—no food, drinking water, or blankets, and sleeping tents had yet to be set up. On their first day in Waimea, the men bought up all the supplies at the little Hayashi Store and set up tents in biting wind and rain.

The 40,000-acres of Parker Ranch grounds were named Camp Tarawa and leased to the United States for $1.00 per year. In early summer 1944, the Second Division sailed away. They would go on to fight at Saipan, Tinian, and Okinawa. Days later, the Fifth Marine Division arrived at Camp Tarawa from California. The Fifth Division trained on Hawai'i Island through December 1944.

This marker was erected at the entrance to Camp Tarawa in 1995. Camp Tarawa was located on the ma uka and ma kai sides of the Upper Road to Kona as it emerges from the center of Waimea toward Waikoloa. [Pacific War Memorial Association]

The sandy beaches from Waikoloa running fifteen miles north to Kawaihae Bay became sites for amphibious training. Battalions trained on ranch lands up at Kahuā, running their jeeps through unharvested sugarcane fields.

The Marines' presence improved life in the cattle town of Waimea (population 400) as well as other surrounding plantation towns. The Second built a dam and a water reservoir and expanded Waimea's limited supply of electricity. They made ice cream for themselves and local children. Waimea's elementary school and little hotel were transformed into modern hospital facilities. Entertainers and hula dancers came to town. Business in and around Waimea boomed. Intense friendships between Big islanders and Marines were forged. Entrepreneurial cooks could hardly supply enough hamburgers. The Fifth Division especially, less exhausted and traumatized than the Second had been, knew how to have a good time. In Honoka'a (nicknamed Honey Cow), Pa'auilo, and as far away as Hāwī in North Kohala, commerce, bars, and prostitution thrived. Waimea women knit warm sweaters for the town's cold days and gave them to Marines. Parker Ranch cowboys staged rodeos. Families invited the Marines to home-cooked meals and to outings to favorite streams and waterfalls. Several freshwater ponds took on the name "Queen's Bath" during those years, named for the real or imagined presence of girlfriends.

Right after Christmas 1944, the Fifth Division Marines departed. To train, they daily climbed the steep hills surrounding Waimea, preparing for a critical battle that might end the Pacific War. Their Big Island hill climbing paid off for the Camp Tarawa Marines who raised the American flag on the summit of Mount Suribachi on Iwo Jima on February 23, 1945, becoming World War II icons. The survivors of Iwo Jima returned to Camp Tarawa for rest and relaxation and to begin training for the imminent invasion of Japan. The people of Waimea welcomed them with open arms. The Japanese surrender ended the war, and the Marine camp closed in December 1945. To honor the Waimea community and Parker Ranch for their wartime welcome, the Fifth Division presented Parker Ranch manager A. H. Carter with a copy of the famous flag-raising photo signed by sixty survivors of the Battle of Iwo Jima.

Life in Waimea went back to its ranching ways, though the war brought many changes. The USO building became classrooms for Parker School. An old hotel and public school used to house nurses and a hospital reopened at Waimea School. The Parker Ranch Museum once housed Division Headquarters and the Officer's Mess.

A stone monument donated by the Exchange Club of Waimea now marks the spot on Highway 190 just outside of the town where Camp Tarawa's main gate welcomed some 50,000 Marines, Navy Corpsmen, and Seabees. In 1995, nearly fifty Camp Tarawa veterans returned for a special reunion with Waimea residents. ■

WORLD WAR II ON MAUI

1. **The Fourth Marine Division at Kokomo. The knoll at the right is still called Giggle Hill, as its peak was the site of off-duty activities of Marines and local girls. [Bren and Fred Bailey Collection]**

2. **Maui residents viewing United States Navy maneuvers through barbed wire strung on South Maui beach. Because of military censorship, photos such as this one are seldom seen. [Bishop Museum]**

World War II not only knocked on Maui's door, it lingered on the lanai. Men in uniform outnumbered local residents four to one.

During World War II, 200,000 soldiers, sailors, Marines, and Seabees flooded the community for training, as well as rest between missions. Some units stayed only a short time, some longer, but each impacted the rural, plantation-oriented community.

The military presence on Maui began in 1940, when the U.S. Navy started construction of a naval air station at the site of the newly built community airport at Puʻunēnē to provide a base for the first military unit to be stationed on Maui, Utility Squadron 3. At the time of the 1941 attack on Pearl Harbor, 150 Navy men and seven officers, plus a few U.S. Army personnel, called Puʻunēnē Naval Air Station home.

"Sub Shells Kahului!" screamed the *Maui News* headline. Luckily, the Japanese submarine that sneaked within range of Kahului on December 15, 1941, had bad aim. Two shells landed in the harbor, and three grazed the Maui Pineapple Company cannery. Once again on December 31, a Japanese submarine wasted its ammunition, first undershooting into the harbor and then overshooting the town in the direction of Puʻunēnē.

Peace of mind took a harder hit. More evidence of Japanese aggression surfaced on December 21, when thirty survivors of a submarine attack on the Matson freighter *Lahaina* came to shore at Spreckelsville after traveling 800 miles in a harrowing eleven-day journey that cost the lives of four crewmen. Maui again directly confronted war in early 1942, when a Japanese torpedo sank the Army transport *Royal T. Frank* within sight of land between Maui and Hawaiʻi Island, killing over twenty men. The ship was transporting draftees from Hilo to Schofield Barracks. A local boat rescued the several dozen survivors and landed them at Hāna.

The advent of war spurred the rapid expansion of the naval air station as a site for the training and staging of carrier air groups. In 1945, 206 officers and 2,465 enlisted men and women were assigned to the station, plus 700 additional men in transient squadrons and 271 aircraft.

Despite its expansion, the naval station at Puʻunēnē proved inadequate to meet the urgent need for training large numbers of pilots and crews required for the Pacific Theater. In response, by early 1943, the Navy trans-

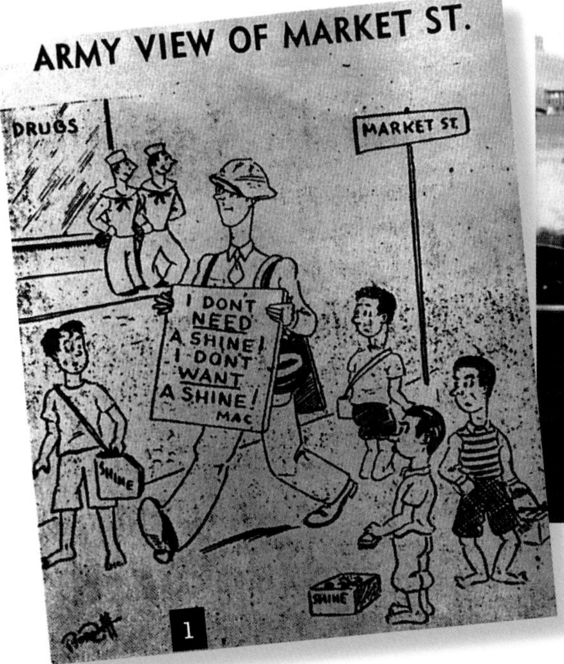

1. A 1942 cartoon appearing in the *Maui News* depicting life on Market Street, Wailuku. [*Maui News*]

2. Navy F6F Grumman Hellcat carrier-based fighters (foreground) and silver SNJ Texan trainers built by North American Aviation (background) at Naval Air Station in Kahului. [Bren and Fred Bailey Collection]

formed yet more cane fields into the Kahului Naval Air Station to provide a training site for more air groups.

Aviators sped through concentrated training, including: daily patrols, predawn launches, torpedo, rocket, and bombing attacks, gunnery firings, carrier landing practices, intercepts, radar and oxygen hops, radar approaches, mine-laying flights, camera and mapping flights, and survival lectures. Mauians lived with the din of airplane engines around the clock.

This intense instruction prepared the Navy men for high-risk assignments in the Pacific. After experiencing the tension of combat, the aviators would once again return to Mau, with elation in their hearts and celebration on their minds. One squadron returned from action in the Solomon islands to see the rooftops around Puʻunēnē carrying messages of welcome spelled out in flowers. The most famous of the Navy air groups used Maui as a staging area, and the Island became well known in naval aviation circles.

The Navy's presence was not limited to Puʻunēnē and Kahului. A Demolition Training Station at Kīhei developed underwater demolition teams and furthered knowledge of antimine cables used on warships. And the Navy and Marines could not have functioned without the aid of four Seabee battalions stationed wherever their construction skills were needed.

Also contributing to the military effort beginning in 1943, a Coast Guard contingent of 500 officers and men kept watch over the port of Kahului. The Coast Guard patrolled piers, regulated fishing, protected sugar shipments, and in cooperation with the Army and Marines, guarded the docks and ships when valuable war cargoes were unloaded.

Then, the Marines landed. Camp Maui, a huge base camp in the Kokomo area of upcountry Maui, was erected in February 1944 as a refuge between Pacific battles for almost 20,000 men of the Fourth Marine Division. The Marines revered 1,600-acre Camp Maui as a site for rest and recreation even though rain fell on many activities including nightly open-air movies.

Maui's varied terrain, from mountain to sea, provided excellent training grounds for these fighting men heading for landings on the beaches of Western Pacific islands at Tinian and Saipan and on cinder-covered Iwo Jima located in the Bonin islands to the east of Japan. Marines trained all over the Island. Day and night, Marines fired at targets with rifles, shot bazookas and machine guns, practiced coordinating land-sea-air at-

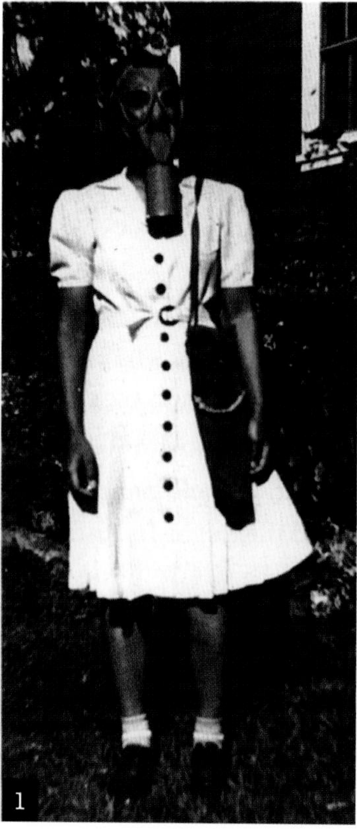

1. A Maui girl wearing gas mask, prepared for a possible invasion of the Island. Even babies were issued gas masks, called bunny masks. [Olivia Pacheco]

HOME EDITION MAUI NEWS

SUB SHELLS KAHULUI!

DAMAGE SLIGHT No Injuries

Niihau Is 'Taken' But Hawaiian Man 'Takes' The Taker

Dusk Attack Witnessed By Many; Cannery Plant Hit

Japanese Pilot Makes Forced Landing After Air Fight; Is Killed

War Fronts In Pacific Are Active

Blackout Is Mother Of Invention

No Casualties In Mauis' First Actual Bombardment

When Shells Dropped On Maui

Residents Remain Calm As Gun Hurls Explosives Into Harbor And Town

Kula Asks $10,000 For 1942 Budget

Rose Bowl Game Set

Two-Man Sub Taken

Schools Reclosed By Order Of Short

EDITORIALS

2. *Maui News* headline in 1941, reporting an attack by a Japanese submarine on December 15. [*Maui News*]

tacks against heavily defended Japanese-held islands, survived rugged jungle training, simulated close-in cave and village fighting, hiked thirteen miles across Haleakalā, and much more.

Workers on Maui's plantations prepared the Marines for the rigors of fighting in the sugar fields of Saipan and Tinian by teaching them how to maneuver through the dense cane and how to fight cane fires.

The Maui Planters Association explained their contributions with the statement, "Uncle Sam's fighting men and the Sugar Industry are Comrades against the Axis!" reminding all that sugar converted to industrial alcohol became explosives, and that sugar gave soldiers essential energy for the challenges of the battlefront.

Other local patriots formed the Maui Volunteers to guard vital installations, to keep peace in plantation camps, and to prepare for possible attack. Army-trained and uniformed in khaki, the men practiced and patrolled after long hours in plantation jobs. Also concerned with the Island's defense, cowboys guarded the vast Maui ranch lands on horseback as members of the Maui Mounted Patrol.

Citizens of Maui could not forget the war for long for there were constant reminders. Military men on leave crowded the streets of every town. Shoeshine boys, restaurants, photo studios, and lei sellers mushroomed in Wailuku and other areas to cater to the military trade. And defense measures radically altered the Island's appearance: camouflage paint coated buildings, including Baldwin High School and Kaʻahumanu Church, barbed wire lined beaches, and blackout paint shrouded windows.

Mauians' eagerness to serve their country surpassed the military's capacity to enlist them. Men of Portuguese, Hawaiian, Puerto Rican, Filipino, Chinese, Caucasian, and Korean ancestry responded readily at the call to arms after Pearl Harbor. Once enlisted, they amassed a memorable record in every branch of the military. Maui's women also served honorably in the Women's Army Corps.

Because so many Japanese American young men flocked to Maui's recruitment office, the Army raised its quota. Those selected from throughout the Islands formed the 442nd Regimental Combat Team.

1. Military recruiting advertisement appearing in the *Maui News*, 1943. *[Maui News]*

2. Lahaina storefront showing photos of Maui servicemen, as encouragement to buying war bonds. [Dorothy Chang]

The Marines won their way into the hearts of the people and became known as "Maui's Own." The sentiment was mutual. When the men of the Fourth Division emerged triumphant at Iwo Jima, they named the first street built there "Maui Boulevard." And, when they returned to Maui after the costly battle, the Maui community turned out en masse at Kahului Harbor to welcome their warriors home. The local community showed their aloha for the last time by providing a heroes' send-off when the Fourth Marine Division departed in November 1945.

The presence of the Army added to the mix of military on Maui. When the war began, its Army contingent consisted of a battalion of local troops of the 299th Infantry of the Hawai'i National Guard. That was soon to change. Early 1942 brought the arrival of the Twenty-Seventh Division, followed by units of the Fortieth Division and the units of the Thirty-Third Division, all of which saw action in the Pacific. The last to arrive was the Ninety-Eighth Mohawk Division. Army units occupied camps at locations throughout Maui, including Kula and the Maui County Fairgrounds. They operated two hospitals, one newly constructed in Waikapū and one based in the former Makawao School. The Army, along with the Navy and the Marines, utilized Maui's forty-seven military sites.

Military life on Maui was not all work. USOs beckoned servicemen at Makawao, Pā'ia, Ha'ikū, Kahului, Wailuku, and Camp Maui. A parade of local hula dancers, singers, and dance bands, as well as big Hollywood names, including Bob Hope, entertained the troops. Sports leagues offered diversion, highlighted by occasional visits from major league baseball players who challenged the servicemen to play ball games.

Local residents generously welcomed military men into their homes between missions. Renowned Maui author Alexa von Tempsky Zabriskie was particularly noted for her hospitality during these years. Zabriskie entertained more than 20,000 officers and men at Erehwon, her ranch located on the slopes of Haleakalā. Maui families were often the last civilians many of these men saw before meeting their deaths in Pacific Island battles.

Surviving Fourth Division Marines returned from battle aboard transports for rest and relaxation on Maui. Some 17,000 of the estimated 100,000 Marines who passed through Maui in 1944–1945 fell as casualties in the faraway battles. In early April 1945, the vic-

torious Fourth Division returned to Camp Maui from the hard-fought battle to take cinder-covered Iwo Jima. On the Fourth of July, the Marines marched in a parade held on the Camp Maui airstrip. At the celebration, the Fourth Division received two Presidential Unit Citations, and the Congressional Medal of Honor was awarded to twelve of the Maui-trained men.

Maui men of every race put their lives on the line for their country. Lieutenant Wilbert Yee spent two years in a German prisoner of war camp, and Staff Sergeant John Gomes Jr. flew on numerous combat missions over Europe as a bombardier. Sergeant Valentine Kekipi earned Maui's first Silver Star for heroic conduct in New Guinea, and Major Gordon Walker received a Navy Cross for courage in the Pacific. One hundred and twenty-four Maui men met death in Europe and in the Pacific in defense of their country and their Island.

The fateful four years of World War II left a legacy for modern-day Maui. Tangible evidence of the Puʻunēnē Naval Air Station remains in view between Kīhei and Puʻunēnē, and concrete pillboxes, bunkers, and bomb casings spot the contemporary landscape from Kula to Mākena. Although the Kahului Naval Air Station is gone, its location is still commonly called Naska, the military contraction for Naval Air Station Kahului. Former members of the Fourth Marine Division keep Camp Maui's memory alive through the Kalapukua Playground, where they have placed a memorial. And the least tangible remnants of the pervasive military presence, but the most important, are the friendships established between local people and military men that are maintained to this day. ■

1. Napoleon Agasid, manager of the Maui branch of the Filipino Federation of America, and a coworker promoting the sale of war bonds in the 1940s. [Napoleon Agasid]

2. Jiro Suzawa of Lahaina at his sendoff to military service, 1943. Suzawa was a member of the highly decorated 442nd Regimental Combat Team, one of many who made the ultimate sacrifice on the battlegrounds of Europe. [Maui Land and Pineapple Company]

WORLD WAR II ON KAUA'I

For Kaua'i's people, the day of the Pearl Harbor attack was an apparently peaceful day off from work at plantation mills and fields, a day following a pattern much in place since the late 1800s. Life on Kaua'i was much simpler then. Only a handful of tourists visited the Island each week, arriving on steamers at Nāwiliwili or by air at Hanapēpē.

Local residents listening to Sunday morning radio broadcasts from Honolulu learned of the Japanese Imperial Navy attack on Pearl Harbor as it was happening. Alan Fayé Jr., then a schoolboy, recalled hearing of the attack as he waited at Burns Field in Hanapēpē for his uncle to return aboard an interisland flight from Honolulu.

"Webley Edwards was on the air and was saying, 'This practice sure looks real! There are airplanes buzzing all around and even the black smoke in the distance looks real.' Just then a bomb blasted a building next to the KGMB radio station and there was a moment of silence . . . followed by, 'Hey, this is no maneuvers, this is the real McCoy!' Minutes later the Kaua'i National Guard arrived in a pickup truck armed to the teeth, ready to hold off the impending invasion. Each Guardsman had a World War I–vintage Springfield rifle and a clip that held five rounds of ammo!"

Later that day, one of the U.S. Navy planes that managed to get airborne during the attack landed at Burns Field to make an emergency refueling stop and immediately took off again. At the Barking Sands airstrip at Mānā north of Waimea, oil drums from Waimea Garage were rolled onto the dirt runway to shut down the field.

Two Japanese pilots flew their Mitsubishi Zeroes over the Forbidden Island of Ni'ihau, seventeen miles southwest of Kaua'i. One crash-landed near the Island's main village, resulting in what became known as the Ni'ihau Incident.

Radio news bulletins broadcast from Līhu'e on radio station KTOH continued during the day (thanks to an oversight by military authorities, who immediately shut down all other radio stations in Hawai'i), confirming that Pearl Harbor had indeed been sneak-attacked by Japanese bombers. On O'ahu, word spread that Kaua'i had been invaded by the Japanese.

Kaua'i's people quickly sprang into action. Charlie Fern, the editor of the *Garden Island* newspaper and operator of Kaua'i's radio station KTOH, rallied the provisional police force. The unit was formed early in 1941, recruiting men from every town and village on Kaua'i in anticipation of war. The men were armed with privately owned rifles and handguns and not a few Ben Franklin Store air guns. By nightfall on December 7, the volunteers took control of every power plant, wa-

WAR DAILY **The Garden Island** WAR DAILY

WED., JAN. 7, 1942

This War In Brief

The Japanese invaders of Luzon today launched a new drive against the American and Filipino troops of General Douglas MacArthur, in the Bataan sector of Zambales province. Washington announced that Japanese bombers have begun a virtual non-stop air attack on the fortress of Corregidor.

Officials of the world powers united against the axis today expressed satisfaction and confidence in an allied victory following President Roosevelt's announcement of war production plans unprecedented in the world's history. These plans call for the construction of 185,000 planes (including 145,000 combat planes), 120,000 tanks, 55,000 anti-aircraft guns, and 18,000,000 tons of merchant shipping before Jan. 1, 1944.

President Roosevelt today added to his war plans with a message to Congress which estimated that the war costs for the 12 months between July 1, 1942 and June 30, 1943 will exceed 56 billion dollars.

Washington officials reported that 45 Japanese bombers launched a second heavy assault on Corregidor Tuesday, pounding the fortress for several hours. The enemy is believed to have lost several planes to American anti aircraft fire. The Japanese meanwhile are attempting to soften strong points of General Douglas MacArthur's positions in preparation for an all out assault, possibly by parachute troops.

The Japanese today acknowledged the loss of a submarine and damage to a cruiser off Davao, where American bombers attacked a large Japanese naval force on Monday.

Japanese armored forces meanwhile pushed ahead on the west Malayan front. The British defenders are battling against five to one odds, according to informed sources. Increased Japanese pressure has forced the British to retire to new lines, between 170 and 200 miles from Singapore. A terrific battle for Kuala Lumpur, the capital of the Federated Malay States, is reported raging in central Malaya. Singapore dispatches indicated that the strongest Allied defense lines would be formed to the south of Kuala Lumpur.

The Chinese Central News Agency reported from Chungking today that Japanese forces are in full retreat after a devastating defeat at Changsha, where the invaders lost 36,000 men.

Japanese bombers which attacked military targets at Amboina, 800 miles north of Darwin, killed three civilians according to a Batavia report.

Tokio reports claimed that British defenses in the Brunei sector of Borneo have been overwhelmed. These reports further alleged that the Japanese are operating 80 oil wells captured in the fighting in Sarawak.

"This production (referring to the number of planes tanks, guns and cargo ships to be built in the next two years) will give the Japanese and the Nazis a little idea of what they accomplished with their attack upon Pearl Harbor." F. D. Roosevelt in his message to Congress.

IT'S MARTIAL LAW

It must be realized on this island that martial law now prevails and that under martial law, all constitutional rights are suspended. The only law now in effect is the law of necesessity.

It is very probable that under martial law, the military government may be required to use private property for the defense of this island. If and when the time permits, the owners of the property will be shown the courtesy of asking their permission. However, there may be many occasions when time does not permit, and the property will be taken over without a formal request.

This is just a warning to the general public on what to expect. The matter of settlement for the use of property is a matter of claims which will be adjusted after the war.

Once again, *martial law is the law of necessity.*

Gets 5 Years

A sentence of five years at hard labor was imposed upon Robert Satoru Wasano of Nawiliwili by Provost Marshal E. J. FitzGerald on January 2 in the Provost court at Lihue.

Wasano pled guilty to having burglarized the E. E. Wall home in Lihue in 1938 at which time he took several articles of jewelry.

His case was one of those scheduled to be tried in the Fifth Circuit court when Martial Law suspended the criminal courts of Hawaii.

Wasano was represented by William Achi as counsel.

Filipinos Can Volunteer

Commissioner Joaquin Elizalde, according to United Press, announced yesterday that Filipinos are eligible to volunteer in the United States Army.

It is reported that thousands have volunteered on the mainland. Commissioner Elizalde urges his countrymen to volunteer their services at the nearest recruiting station.

BLACKOUT HOURS:
6 p.m. to 6 a.m.

Yun H. Lai Fined $100

A fine of $100 and a one month's suspension of his license was imposed upon Yun How Lai of Kapaa by Provost Marshal E. J. FitzGerald on Tuesday morning in the Provost court at Lihue.

Yun Lai was convicted of maintaining a butcher shop at Kapaa in an unsanitary condition. He was represented by Eugene Aiu as counsel.

The Provost Marshal stipulated that the fine of $100 must be paid within 48 hours.

KAUAI'S SNUFFY SMITH SEZ:

Yep, I ben plum mad fer a week. I ben tellin' the Kauai Chamber of Commerce thet we-uns got to complaint to Tokyo fer leavin' Kauai out'en her brags.

Jumpin' jeepers, some'un beat 'em to it—mebbe it wer that Equal Rights commission. Enyhow, whodone it must a scairt them Nipponese outa ther senses fer las nite the Tokyo radio sez loud like:

"Our warcraft shelled and completely demolished important military objectives at Nawiliwili, Kauai."

USCGC USS *Tiger* crew posing in front of the Captain Cook Monument in Waimea on the Island of Kaua'i, 1945. [Unknown source]

terworks and bridges, and all intersections along Kūhiō and Kaumuali'i Highway. Word spread quickly among the 35,000 Kauaians, and by noon an ambulance corps was mobilized. Many Kaua'i women, trained as nurses' aides by the Red Cross, went to hospitals to prepare to accept casualties.

After the excitement of the Pearl Harbor attack died down, the Island quietly and quickly did what it could to prepare for a possible invasion. Young schoolchildren worked gardens, high schoolers joined them and also strung barbed wire along beaches. Japanese Americans, many of whom were excluded from the defense work, formed groups such as the Sons of Mokihana to give blood, clear kiawe, and other important but mundane work; Filipino plantation workers were formed into military units, drilled hard to be battle ready, and became eager to join the regular Army. Plantations provided heavy equipment, electricity, and grew hundreds of acres of sweet potatoes, cabbage, and other foodstuffs to ensure a food supply for the Island. Newspaper editor Fern began to chronicle the war through updates of Island events and insightful editorials that in retrospect seemed to aim at keeping a cohesive spirit going among the Island's various racial groups.

Once the war started, everyone was fingerprinted and issued registration cards, along with gas masks and special cloth "bunny masks" complete with little rabbit ears for toddlers and infants. Civilian patrols began to scan the air and sea for signs of attack, and more than a few false alerts of "mysterious lights" and spottings of Japanese submarines were reported along the beaches during the blackouts that were held every night.

Three weeks after Pearl Harbor, the Island's fear of invasion stirred again when, at 1:30 a.m. on December 30, a Japanese submarine sitting about four miles offshore lobbed about fifteen three-inch shells at targets in

Nāwiliwili lighting up Kalapakī Bay with bright flares. Damage was minor, just a small cane fire and shrapnel holes in the second story of a home overlooking the bay. Termed a "punch in the nose" by many, the incident would be Kaua'i's first and last Japanese attack of the war.

On Easter Sunday of 1942, the first mainland troops to be stationed on Kaua'i during World War II arrived. It was a rainy day that turned the dirt roads of the Island into slippery obstacles. The troops of the Army's Twenty-Seventh Division spread around the Island in trucks driven sometimes by female members of Kaua'i's Women's Motor Corps. Many were fresh from New York, Pittsburgh, and other big East Coast cities. They found Kaua'i as exotic as the South Pacific. Local pidgin and place names were a mysterious foreign language for the mainland troops while local folk were as mystified by some of the troops' urban accents. Ray H. Smith, the nine-year-old son of Kōloa Union Church minister Howard A. Smith, a former missionary to China, found the accent of friendly Brooklyn troops, who tipped him royally for fetching them cans of pineapple juice, "the strangest pidgin I ever heard."

At the head of the Twenty-Seventh was the famous "Fightin' Sixty-Ninth," members of New York's highly decorated, mostly Irish 165th Infantry.

The troops strung thousands of rolls of barbed wire and dug machine-gun and mortar positions. They also ran armed motor and radio patrols and worked with the police and fire departments and the telephone company. The Twenty-Seventh Division stayed on-island for eight months, fortifying the entire Island from Kekaha to Hā'ena. Along with local help, the soldiers constructed 150 concrete pillboxes.

Feeling more secure with thousands of regular Army troops pouring in, daily life became a routine shaped by martial law, tight rationing of gas and other goods, food shortages, and a territory-wide blackout each evening. However, news of Japanese victories in Asia and the western Pacific, underscored by unofficial word that a sizable Japanese attack force had sailed, possibly to invade Hawai'i, created a mood of uncertainty.

While the civilian population was kept mostly in the dark about what was unfolding, military authorities feared an amphibious invasion might come ashore at beaches offering strategic openings into and across the heart of the low-lying sections of the Island. Mountainous Kōke'e was decided upon as the site of last retreat, a place where guerrilla warfare might hold off Japanese invaders indefinitely.

Promising to fight alongside the mainland troops to the last, a home guard, the Kaua'i Volunteers, was formed. Three battalions were sworn in: one from Kekaha to Hanapēpē, one from Kalāheo to Līhu'e, and one from Kapa'a to Kīlauea.

On March 9, 1942, over 2,400 men enrolled. However, men of Japanese ancestry were denied enrollment.

All the Kaua'i Volunteers were eighteen and over, with many Filipinos enthusiastically joining, glad to help their countrymen who were then desperately holding off Japanese invaders at Bataan and other combat fronts in their homeland. The volunteers supplied their own uniforms: dark blue shirt, khaki pants, a flat helmet, and a khaki jacket. Their insignia was a distinctive chevron with a white capital K sitting inside a dark blue capital V sewn on the left shoulder of their jackets. Night drills and four hours' training each Sunday, plus practice with real rifles, pistols, and machine guns soon honed their military skills.

The volunteers worked regular jobs, mostly on plantations during the week, and fell in on Sundays for training. Special forces included a mounted detachment of mostly Hawaiian and Portuguese paniolo cowboys formed by Captain Alan Fayé Sr. of Kekaha to patrol ma uka ranch lands and to act as forward scouts and spies in case of invasion. Many volunteers made do with Kaua'i-style weapons, including a regulation Filipino-style bolo cane knife sharpened down to a razor-blade edge.

Japanese American men from the Island were anxious to serve in the armed forces, but they had to wait until 1943 for their chance. Though the largest single ethnic group then on Kaua'i, questions lingered about the loyalty to America of the Issei and Nisei, first- and second-generation Japanese Americans.

Some 1,600 Japanese American families in May 1942 joined the the Kaua'i Morale Committee. The group purchased over $800,000 in war bonds, formed the Kiawe Corps to clear the thorny wood from ex-

1. Women's Air Raid Defense (WARD) members at work in the interceptor room, O'ahu, 1943: (left to right) Evelyn O'Brien, Betty Cornwell, Daisy Williams, Ann Simms, and Captain Greco. [U.S. Army Signal Corps/University of Hawai'i War Records Depository/HWRD1227]

2. Women's Army Corps Private Harriet Lum of Kapa'a, Kaua'i, packs her duffle bag for her trip to the Mainland Army Post where she will receive her basic training. She enlisted in the WAC in Honolulu, Hawai'i, in November 1944. [U.S. Army Signal Corps/University of Hawai'i War Records Depository/HWRD1367]

posed coastal areas, plus volunteered and generously donated funds to the Red Cross, USO, and Welfare funds.

Beginning in March of 1943, over 760 of Kaua'i's military-age Japanese American men filed for induction. Most went to the European theater and a few to the Pacific battlefields and islands to serve as language translators and in intelligence operations. In all, of the 1,300 Kaua'i men who went off to war, 48 died in service, mostly in the Italian campaign as members of the U.S. Army's famous AJA 442nd Regimental Combat team, the most decorated World War II outfit in all the U.S. armed forces.

The Japanese Americans on Kaua'i also felt the threat of being interned, as were most of California's Japanese Americans, in lonely, isolated camps mostly in cold Rocky Mountain locations far from the coast. Thankfully, only one percent of Kaua'i's Japanese people were taken into custody, those being mostly alien residents who had associations with the Japanese consulate.

Kaua'i men joining the armed forces and leaving the Island saw action in virtually all theaters of the war, from Bataan to Europe, as members of all the services and the Merchant Marine.

The Island's women also had adventures during the war, serving in organizations such as the Women's Air Raid Defense. These "shuffleboard pilots" included high school girls whose job was to plot, on a large tabletop map, the strategic position of the Army Air Corp's Seventy-Eighth Fighter Squadron flying out of Barking Sands field.

The threat of a new Japanese attack and invasion, likely first landing on Kaua'i, the main Island nearest Japan, was a daily fear even after the Twenty-Seventh Division arrived. That attack came in early June, in waters near Midway, over 1,000 miles to the northwest of Kaua'i. For three tense days, civilian and military defense groups were put on "all-out," twenty-four-hour-a-day watches, ready to take up well-rehearsed inland evacuation plans for the Island's women and children. Unconfirmed stories circulated on Kaua'i that carrier planes with bullet holes in their fuselages had refueled at Barking Sands during the battle.

A wave of exultation swept all of Hawai'i on June 5, when word came of a smashing victory at Midway by the American forces. Over twenty Japanese ships, including four aircraft carriers, 275 aircraft, and 4,800 men, were lost by the Japanese. Had victory gone the other way, it was likely Kaua'i would have been invaded before summer, mostly to capture its airfields for use as a base for attacks against the sizable U.S. military force on O'ahu.

The Midway win was termed crucial, but not decisive, by the military. The threat of a Japanese invasion remained ominous, and fortification work continued unabated. By August 1942, nearly 15,000 troops shipped from the mainland had swelled the Island's population count as California's Fortieth Division joined the Twenty-Seventh Division. Most of these two division's forces departed in October for combat training at Schofield Barracks in preparation for the island-jumping battles in the western Pacific. They were replaced by men of the Thirty-Third Division, mostly from Chicago and the Midwest.

By mid-1943, with the Pacific War fronts now far from Kaua'i's shores, tensions eased and a regular schedule of Kaua'i Volunteer drills, war bond fund-raising drives, and live USO entertainment became the norm. With concrete bunkers in place and barbed wire strung along all exposed beaches, the mission of the military bases was switched to "training divisions for combat operations." Realistic grass huts, bamboo bridges, and jungle defenses used by the Japanese in the tropical Pacific were set up by the Marines in Nā Pali valleys, behind Moloa'a and Hanalei, and near Wailua Homesteads to give over 15,000 troops a taste of what to expect when they hit the beach in the Solomons, Guadalcanal, and other treacherous Japanese strongholds. Amphibious landings with cover by speedy PT boats were also staged.

Entertainment for the troops abounded at more than a half-dozen USO clubs, with acts such as homegrown Hawaiian musicians and hula dancers performing at Hanalei, Kapa'a, Līhu'e, Nāwiliwili, Kalaheo, Kōloa, Hanapēpē, and Waimea. The most memorable entertainers were celebrity visitors, including Bob Hope, big-mouthed comedian Joe E. Brown, and an all-star Seventh Air Force baseball team, including Joe DiMaggio.

Kaua'i's people generally got along well with the troops. Many mainland troops saw it as a stroke of luck to be stationed on Kaua'i and other outer Islands, away from the more formal bases on O'ahu. And while there was some friction when mainland servicemen dated local girls, civilian-military problems were minimal. The servicemen generally found a surplus of aloha spirit during their time on Kaua'i. Many were taken on tours of the Island's scenic and historic spots. Local homes were open to the mostly young men, many of whom were away from their own homes for the first time.

Kaua'i's last large influx of troops was the Ninety-Eighth Division, made up of draftees rather than prewar regulars, who arrived in April 1944. A sign that perhaps the war was winding down came in August, when the training centers were shut down. From then to V-J Day in the late summer of 1945, only a token garrison guarded Kaua'i. Altogether, more than 40,000 mainland soldiers passed through the Island during the war.

The years of World War II brought great changes to Kaua'i. Many of the Island's rural towns were inundated with GIs from the mainland, some of whom married local girls or moved back to Kaua'i once their war service was completed.

Kaua'i's Japanese Americans and Filipino Americans also reached new levels of achievement through serving their country both on the Island and overseas.

The generation coming of age on Kaua'i at the opening of the war entered a world of new opportunities unavailable, probably unthinkable, to their parents and grandparents. New friends, marrying mainland and overseas women, and traveling to places far from home, lured many away for good. The days of plantation paternalism were over, small businesses flourished with the number of restaurants and shops that had opened to service the military. The pickup of the economy also shifted the commercial center of the Island from the west side to Līhu'e, where the port of Nāwiliwili and Līhu'e Airport were now the gateways to Kaua'i. ■

THE 442ND REGIMENTAL COMBAT TEAM

The actual date these Nisei soldiers were to leave Honolulu for Oakland, California, was a military secret. Several days after the official departure ceremony, they were awakened early and taken by the O‘ahu Railway to ‘A‘ala Park. Shouldering their heavy duffel bags from the station to the ship docked at the harbor, they expected a quiet farewell from their beloved Islands. However, all the streets were lined with families and friends who had gotten word of the "secret" departure from the "coconut wireless." This unofficial sendoff was an emotional moment they carried with them halfway around the world. [National Archives]

Hawai‘i's Very Special Regiment

Americans of Japanese Ancestry (AJAs) were caused great difficulty by the Imperial Japanese Navy's attack on Pearl Harbor. Many of them in California and other mainland states were interned, quickly dispossessed, and moved to relocation camps. But for the 160,000 Japanese residing in Hawai‘i, most of whom were U.S. citizens, internment was impractical. There were not enough ships available to send them to camps on the mainland, and it would have been impossible to intern one-third of the entire population of Hawai‘i.

Still, the military remained uncomfortable with the possibility of a Japanese invasion of the Hawaiian Islands at a time when the population of Hawai‘i was so largely Japanese. As well, there were 1,300 AJAs on duty in Hawai‘i's two national guard battalions. To discharge all of the AJAs was a military luxury that could not be afforded at the time. The military's solution was to separate the Japanese contingent, forming the Hawaiian Provisional Infantry Battalion, composed of 1,406 Nisei (second-generation Japanese) soldiers. During the Battle of Midway in June 1942, the soldiers were sent to Camp McCoy in Wisconsin. There they were treated with considerable friendliness by people of the nearby towns. Later they

Hawai'i's 422nd is off to the war in a ceremony at 'Iolani Palace on March 28, 1943. Nisei volunteers in the Army spent only a short time at a Schofield Barracks "Tent City" before being shipped out to basic training in Wisconsin and Mississippi. Recognizing that these young men had family members who wanted to wish them a special aloha before leaving, the military arranged the farewell ceremony. A huge crowd of friends and relatives watched 2,000 new soldiers march smartly down King Street, then assemble on the palace grounds for final speeches, an official photograph, and to receive lei and small envelopes of cash as traditional gifts. [Hawai'i State Archives]

were transferred to Camp Shelby in Mississippi where racial hostility toward them at times was intense because of their "color." The Hawaiian Provisional Infantry Battalion was renamed the 100th Battalion and after training was sent to the battlefields of North Africa and Italy.

Later the War Department authorized the formation of an all–AJA fighting unit and put out a call for Hawai'i volunteers in early 1943 after reclassifying the men who had been tagged at draft boards as 4-C, or enemy aliens.

The original appeal was for 1,500 volunteers, but within a month over 9,000 young AJAs flocked to recruitment centers across Hawai'i. Some 2,645 were selected to serve, and they formed the core of the 442nd Infantry Regimental Combat Team. On June 11, 1944, the 442nd joined the 100th Battalion north of Rome and eventually absorbed that unit. In the French and Italian campaigns, more than 650 AJA officers and enlisted men lost their lives, and more than 4,500 were wounded. Many of these casualties were from Hawai'i.

The 442nd Regimental Combat Team served in battles fought against the European Axis powers in Italy, France, and Germany. The heroic "Go for Broke" deter-

1. Volunteer enlistees draped in lei. March 27, 1943. [Bishop Museum]

2. A group of young men about to leave Kona to enter military service during World War II. Note the lei, farewell gifts from family and friends. Date unknown. [Kona Historical Society]

3. From back of print: S. Agata Di Goti, Italy: 2nd Lieutenants Hideo Kaichi, Yutaka K. Yoshida and Bobuo F. Tanigawa, all from the Hawaiian Islands and veterans of the 442nd Regimental Combat Team, just after they received their bars after completion of a twelve week course at the leadership and battle school. [U.S. Army Signal Corps/University of Hawai'i War Records Depository/HWRD1443]

mination of the men of the 442nd led them to become the most highly decorated unit in the history of the U.S. Army when comparing the length of time served and number of men in the unit.

The combat record of these young AJAs is unequalled in the annals of American military history. They fought valiantly in Italy and France. Their casualty rate was three times higher than the average combat unit. The combined units won seven Presidential Unit Citations and nearly 6,000 other medals were awarded to individual soldiers. The 442nd became known as the Purple Heart Battalion.

The men of the 442nd returned to Hawai'i with a new heightened status in Hawai'i's social structure because of their valor in war and their loyalty forever established. They had traveled; they had seen much and suffered much. Soon, they would enter politics and help transform Hawai'i's politics. Men of the 442nd, including Senator Daniel Inouye of Honolulu, a Congressional Medal of Honor winner, were elected to county, state, and national offices running as reform Democrats, playing a leading role in gaining statehood in 1959. ■

Americans of Japanese descent of the 442nd Regimental Combat Team, 100th Infantry Battalion, in bivouac prepare to go into front lines for their first contact with the Germans in France. T/5 Teroo Goma, Honoka'a; Private Nolan Miyazake, Wailua, and Private Kunio Ogawa, Kahului, write letters and read. [U.S. Army Signal Corps/University of Hawai'i War Records Depository/HWRD1438]

Varsity Victory Volunteers

The Varsity Victory Volunteers played a key role in the formation of the 100th Infantry Battalion and the all-Nisei 442nd Infantry Regimental Combat Team. In the days after the attack on Pearl Harbor, members of the University of Hawai'i's Reserve Officers' Training Corps (ROTC) were ordered to join the Hawai'i Territorial Guard (HTG). About 150 of the students guarded docks, electric plants, and hospitals in place of Army and National Guard soldiers assigned to beaches to fight off a possible invasion by Japan. During the weeks of uncertainty following the Pearl Harbor attack, no one questioned the loyalty of the Americans of Japanese Ancestory (AJA) ROTC men. However, in late January 1942, these students were relieved of their HTG duty due to suspicion about their loyalty to the United States rooted in lingering racial prejudice dating back to the nineteenth century. Regrouping by late February, with support from community leaders led by Hung Wai Ching, about 170 students formed the Varsity Victory Volunteers. The "Triple-V" became a volunteer labor battalion for the U.S. Army Corps of Engineers stationed at Schofield Barracks. The Triple-V worked building military roads, painting buildings, and digging ditches, proving their loyalty and gaining acceptance by the soldiers at Schofield Barracks. Buying war bonds, donating blood, and helping with community organizations also gained them notice.

In early 1943, with the support of President Franklin Delano Roosevelt and his wife Eleanor, who learned of the Triple-V's record, the U.S. War Department changed the 4-C (enemy alien) draft board classification of AJAs, opening the door for the Triple-V students and all qualified Nisei men to serve in the U.S. armed forces. The 442nd was soon formed, with many of the Varsity Victory Volunteers signing up. Some of the students joined the Military Intelligence Service, where they used their Japanese language skills in translating captured documents and interrogating POWs.

THE NI'IHAU INCIDENT

Today a diorama illustrating the Ni'ihau Incident stands in the Pacific Aviation Museum located on Ford Island in Pearl Harbor. On display is the twisted metal remains of a Mitsubishi A6M2 Zero fighter plane, weathered by over sixty years of exposure to salty air and red dirt. Keith Robinson and his brother Bruce Robinson, who co-own Ni'ihau Island, donated the destroyed Zero. A restored Zero, on display nearby, is painted with the correct colors, insignias, and identification numbers of the crashed Zero. The display draws "I never knew about this..." comments from the tens of thousands of visitors who tour the Pacific Aviation Museum each year, helping to memorialize this once obscure but always intriguing chapter in the world-changing Pearl Harbor attack saga.

Wreckage of A6M2 Zero Nishikaichi crashed in a Ni'ihau field. [U.S. Army, James Lansdale, Wikimedia Commons]

Back in 1941, in the early afternoon following the attack on Pearl Harbor, the Ni'ihau Incident began near Pu'uwai village on the southwest coast of remote Ni'ihau Island. Local residents spotted two fighter planes flying over their 70-square-mile island. No one on Ni'ihau yet knew of the attack on Pearl Harbor.

Though just 120 miles from the action that day on O'ahu and 17 miles across the Kaulakahi Channel from Kaua'i, Ni'ihau was the Forbidden Island, a native Hawaiian enclave with one foot in the nineteenth century. Owner Aylmer Robinson allowed no uninvited visitors to travel to Ni'ihau due to a prior introduction of a serious illness by a visitor. Ni'ihau's 125 or so mostly native Hawaiian residents spoke Hawaiian as a first language. Community life was based around their Hawaiian church. Contemporary Hawaiian life was a twelve-hour whaleboat paddle away on Kaua'i. The Ni'ihauans' Christian beliefs were reflected in their community standards. Drinking, smoking, and gambling were forbidden. In their close-knit society they led a hearty life, fishing, working on the Ni'ihau ranch, working as beekeepers, picking the famed Ni'ihau shells to string lei. Most Western ways and modern comforts like electricity were absent.

This quiet Sunday afternoon, the Pearl Harbor drama reached out to terrorize them. The Ni'ihau Incident became a unique chapter in Hawaiian history, becoming a tale of "locality and Hawaiian character, that could never have occurred anywhere else," as author Blake Clark described it in *Reader's Digest* magazine.

The Incident began when one of the single-seater attack planes with a red circle visible on its wings fell from the sky and sank offshore. Meanwhile another Zero, trailing black smoke from an oil leak, made a landfall, crash landing near the main Ni'ihau village of Pu'uwai. Japanese Navy pilots attacking Pearl Harbor were told to land on a west side beach on Ni'ihau if unable to return to their carriers cruising north of Oahu and Kaua'i. The Japanese submarine I-74 would patrol that coast and pick up crashed pilots.

Aylmer Robinson spent years having his men plow furrows across Ni'ihau fields to prevent such a landing. Husky Ni'ihau cowboy Hawila "Howell" Kaleohano spotted the crash from the front porch of his plantation-style home. The Zero came to a stop in an arid, weedy field near Hawila's home, twisting the propeller of the single-engine plane and smashing its landing gear. Imperial Japanese Navy Air Service pilot Shigenori Nishikaichi, about twenty-one years old, sat still in the cockpit as Hawila approached.

At about 9 a.m., in the second wave attack on Pearl Harbor, Nishikaichi had taken off from the Imperial Navy carrier *Hiryū* to strafe Bellows Field in Windward O'ahu. With his fuel running low, he nursed his dam-

aged plane northwest with instructions to force land if need be on Ni‘ihau, an island the Japanese pilots were told was uninhabited. There he was to await pickup by an I-Class rescue submarine.

The pilot pulled his revolver on Kaleohano. Undaunted, the Ni‘ihauan ripped the pilot out of his harness, pulling the pilot's gun away and grabbing a packet of papers, including a map of O‘ahu that the Japanese flyer frantically attempted to stuff inside his shirt.

Nonopapa residents encircled the Zero. They were at home from ranching and other jobs on Sunday, a sabbath day of rest for them, and gathered around the downed Zero. The pilot surrendered. He was allowed to wander around Nonopapa unguarded and replied in vague answers in simple English words to questions about who he was and why he landed on Ni‘ihau.

Shigenori Nishikaichi. [Unknown, Wikimedia Commons]

Yoshio Harada, a Nisei who had worked on Ni‘ihau for three years, was "summoned and spoke with the pilot in Japanese, but was not able to learn the circumstances of the visit," according to an Army report of the incident.

On Tuesday and Wednesday, the Zero pilot, accompanied by Harada and Ishimatsu Shintani, a Japanese national married to a Ni‘ihauan woman, went to Ki‘i Landing on the northeast tip of Ni‘ihau, where a whaleboat was stationed. However, the winter seas were too rough to make the passage to Kaua‘i's west coast.

On Thursday, Harada "complained to the Hawaiians, stating that it was a mistake that the two Ni‘ihau Japanese were selected as guards for the pilot." They were relieved.

On Friday, Shintani mysteriously sought the pilot's papers from Kaleohano, attempting to bribe him with $200 in cash, a lot of money on Ni‘ihau, saying he wanted to burn the papers and that his life was being threatened by Nishikaichi.

That night, events turned violent. Harada and the pilot broke into Shintani's home. Failing to find the papers, they took a handful of Ni‘ihauans hostage using the pilot's pistol, which they stole from Kaleohano's house. Harada armed himself with a shotgun purloined from Aylmer Robinson's Ni‘ihau residence.

At midnight the pilot powered up the radio in his Zero and sent a message in Japanese that went unanswered. Overhearing the pilot, the Ni‘ihauans were worried that armed aid from a Japanese ship might be on the way.

Following a community prayer meeting, most of the Ni‘ihauans scattered to remote beaches or into the mountains. Some climbed to the top of the 1,281-foot-high peak Pānī‘au to attempt to signal Kaua‘i using kerosene lamps and reflectors.

Nishikaichi lit his Zero on fire at 3 a.m. on Saturday and burned Kaleohano's nearby home where he believed the papers taken from him by Kaleohana were hidden.

Six men, including Kaleohano, all strong paddlers, went to Ki‘i Landing and launched a whaleboat, heading as fast as possible for Waimea.

On Saturday, December 13 the pilot and Harada spotted respected Ni‘ihau elder Bene "Benehakaka" Kanahele and his wife Ella near the beach at Nonopapa. Ella was held hostage, and Bene was ordered to search for Kaleohano, the pilot still desperately seeking to recover his papers. Harada threatened Kanahele, telling him he would be killed along with the villagers if he failed to find Kaleohano. Kanahele departed but soon returned, knowing that Kaleohano was in the whaleboat rowing to Kaua‘i.

At about 10 a.m., Kanahele acted fast, sensing Harada and Nishikaichi were tired, having been up overnight. As the pilot handed Aylmer Robinson's shotgun to Harada, Bene and Ella lunged at him. The pilot

pulled out his revolver, which he had tucked away in his boot. Ella grabbed his arm. The pilot held on and haphazardly fired three times at Bene, shooting him in his upper thigh, groin, and stomach. Bene recovered, bodily picked up the pilot, and smashed his head on a lava rock wall. Ella finished him off with a rock. Harada, shocked, turned the shotgun on himself, firing twice into his abdomen. Soon after, he died.

An Army expedition from Kauaʻi arrived early Sunday afternoon. They returned overnight to Port Allen, the main harbor on Kauaʻi's West Side, aboard the U. S. Coast Guard's Lighthouse Service tender *Kukui.* Aboard were Shintani with Harada's wife and child, who were immediately jailed by the Army. Bene was treated and hospitalized in Waimea.

News of the Kanaheles' exploits, and Bene's bedside photo, garnered front-page coverage in Honolulu. Wire services picked up the story and news of the Niʻihau Incident and its hero, the first American civilian to receive a medal in World War II, spread across the nation, boosting morale in the wake of America's greatest military disaster. Bene's quote, about the third shot by Nishikaichi hitting him, "That's when I got mad," became wartime slang in Hawaiʻi. President Roosevelt later awarded Kanahele the Medal of Merit, the top medal for heroism by a civilian, and the Purple Heart. The snappy hapa-haole Hawaiian tune "Couldn't Take Niʻihau No-How" brought the tale of the Niʻihau Incident into folklore.

In February 1942, President Franklin Delano Roosevelt issued Executive Order #9066, interning over 100,000 Japanese Americans, mostly residents of the Pacific Coast. Seemingly, the Niʻihau Incident didn't influence Roosevelt's decision. Federal Bureau of Investigation director J. Edgar Hoover did send a report on the incident to Roosevelt, but not until March 1942, according to a Niʻihau Incident segment aired on the PBS-TV show *History Detectives.*

A wartime cenotaph memorial column honoring Nishikaichi, misstating that he died on Oʻahu during the Pearl Harbor attack, stands in his hometown of Hashihama. The column was erected prior to the notification of his family in 1956 of the circumstances of the Niʻihau Incident. His ashes were returned to his family. ■

SAILORS, SOLDIERS, AIRMEN, AND MARINES ON LEAVE

As the armed forces of the United States rebounded from the devastation of the Pearl Harbor attack, Hawai'i soon surpassed California as the western front of the nation in the Pacific War.

Hawai'i, the Crossroads of the Pacific, became the training ground, transport stopover, and staging area for a constant flow of tens of thousands of soldiers, sailors, airmen, and Marines heading out to Pacific Island land and sea battles. The supply lines of the Pacific War reached back to the huge supply centers set up on O'ahu and to the shipyard at Pearl Harbor—both requiring a massive infusion of workers from the mainland US.

Granting days of leave was the prime way military authorities kept up the morale of the multitudes of young men and women serving in or transiting Hawai'i. Off base, they had the freedom to roam around Honolulu and rural O'ahu as long as they were back on duty at the required date and time.

For the servicemen and defense workers based on O'ahu, downtown Honolulu—especially Hotel Street—and Waikīkī Beach became favorite haunts. By 1943, it was estimated that upwards of 30,000 daily visited the Hotel Street bars, such as the Hubba Hubba Club, nearby movie theaters, lei sellers, Wo Fat's and other Chinatown restaurants and curio stores, and, of course, the houses of ill-repute.

In downtown Honolulu and Waikīkī, many hotel facilities were used for military rest and recreation. Several USO clubs were opened in Honolulu, with the former House of Mitsukoshi department store transformed into the Victory Club. Daily social gatherings were always popular with Island girls who danced an estimated six million times with servicemen at the Victory Club alone. At the Army-Navy YMCA in downtown Honolulu in December of 1943, these soldiers and sailors enjoyed the grace and beauty of a young hula dancer. [University of Hawai'i War Records Depository]

Local boys shined shoes and fetched Cokes to make some change serving the servicemen and shipyard workers. Many locally owned businesses thrived. Local-military altercations did arise, especially from mainland men unaccustomed to the multiethnic makeup of Hawai'i and the fact that men outnumbered women 100 to 1 once the war effort was in full force. Clamping down problems was a strict curfew blackout from twilight to dawn that limited many leave activities to daylight hours.

At Waikīkī, the Army's USO club hosted big-band orchestras and singers, entertaining the troops night and day. On Waikīkī Beach, concertina wire, strung to ward off invaders, and imposition of martial law caused many beachboys to find other jobs if they hadn't already joined the military. The landmark pink Royal Hawaiian Hotel was closed to tourists but served as an "R&R" rest and relaxation place for submariners.

USO clubs dotted Maui, Hawai'i Island, and Kaua'i. Months-long training regimes prepping for specific Pacific Island battles such as Tarawa and Iwo Jima kept companies of soldiers and Marines on island for months. While lacking the big city attractions of Honolulu, the Islands' rural hospitality and the aloha spirit these troops found created many lifelong friendships with local families. Heartfelt sorrow was shown when a young Marine or soldier with close ties to a local family died on a faraway beachhead.

1. Directly across from the Army-Navy YMCA Club was the infamous Black Cat Cafe, where soldiers and sailors found less reputable activities available. In the early years of the war, the hours of operation for Honolulu bars were restricted to the afternoon. This unfortunately led to an increased amount of public drunkenness as servicemen rushed to fill up on their quota during the restricted hours of operation. One member of the Honolulu Liquor Commission counted seventeen drunks one afternoon as he walked along half a block in downtown. In the course of fifteen minutes he counted three fistfights. When the bars were allowed to stay open until 7 p.m., late in 1943, not all drinking establishments took advantage of the extended hours. The rationing of liquor was very restrictive, with a permit required for three quarts of wine, one case of beer, or one quart of other liquor per week. [Bishop Museum]

2. At the outbreak of the war in 1941, the United Service Organizations, or USO, expanded its operations to five Islands, as over fifty clubs provided entertainment and relaxation to Army and Navy personnel. The Army and Navy YMCA at Hotel and Richards Streets was renamed the USO Army and Navy Club, with hundreds of activities offered every month, ranging from ballroom dancing classes to silent movies. Buses carrying military personnel from a number of posts dropped off their passengers directly in front of the club, which also offered overnight accommodations. [Hawai'i State Archives]

Hotel Street at War

They left Wu Fat's at ten-thirty....They decided to take a taxi out. They dodged catty corner across Hotel to the GI taxi stand in front of the Japanese woman-barber shop and fell in at the end of the mob that was jamming the cab stand almost as badly as the other mob had jammed the bar. Everything was jammed, even the Japanee woman-barber shop had a waiting line.

The cab was moving slowly in the traffic up Hotel Street that was lit up like a carnival. They passed the arcade two doors down from the Army-Navy Y, where a mob was shooting electric eye machine guns at lighted planes or waiting to get their picture taken with their arm drunkenly around the...Japanee hula girl against a canvas backdrop of Diamond Head and palms. Something to Send Home, the sign on the photograph booth said.

The cab moved at a walking pace past the crowded hotdog stand next door to the Y where a bunch waited to use the dime automatic photograph machine, their mass overflowing onto the already jam-packed sidewalk. Then on past the dark palm studded lawn on the Y itself, with the Black Cat across the street and also overflowing. A number of drunks lay passed out on the Y lawn.

James Jones, *From Here to Eternity*
(N.Y.: Scribner's, 1951)

Downtown Honolulu movie houses, such as the Hawaii Theater, were so popular that the military government adjusted the evening curfew to accommodate the film schedule. Not only did Hollywood movies help soldiers forget the realities of war, but the theaters were air-conditioned. [Baker-Van Dyke Collection]

During the war, the U.S. military established bases, shoreline defense systems, training areas and recreation centers throughout the Islands. At Māla Wharf, once located between Lahaina and Kā'anapali, Maui, Navy personnel took over as most of Hawai'i's harbors came under control of the armed forces. [Nakamoto Art Studio]

Ray Jerome Baker: Waikīkī's Wartime Portrait Photographer

With the outset of World War II, renowned Hawai'i photographer Ray Jerome Baker, who kept a photo studio in Waikīkī, and his fellow Honolulu photographers found themselves working day and night taking portraits of servicemen based in or passing through Hawai'i. Under ordinary circumstances, few of these men would have had their pictures taken. But as they were heading into Pacific War battle zones, they faced an uncertain future. Encouraged by requests for photos from their parents, wives, and sweethearts, they kept the studios busy with appointments.

Some of these young men did not come back. Baker sometimes would receive letters from their family and relatives requesting copies of the photos he'd taken while they were in Honolulu. He promptly looked through his files and sent them any additional proofs or negatives. ■

Men of Our Armed Forces

A Study in Faces of Fighting Men

by Ray Jerome Baker, 1945

When, on December 7, 1941, Hawaii, land of green mountains and purple valleys, of sunshine and flowers, was attacked, it at first seemed incredible that war had come to this peaceful community. The ever presence of rainbows and blue seas, of gaiety and laughter belied the possibility of such a catastrophe. Gradually the brutal facts emerged and it became obvious serious times were ahead. The large, but unrevealed, number of casualties at Pearl Harbor convinced everybody that our armed forces faced a harsh, relentless and determined enemy which had spent years in preparing for the attack. It was not long until these peaceful Islands became an armed fortress functioning as a spearhead in the attack on the enemy to the west. It was under the stress and deep concern of these conditions that this series of portraits of MEN OF OUR ARMED FORCES began.

Immediately following the Pearl Harbor assault the conquest of other Pacific Islands took place and within a few months vast territory had fallen into the hands of the enemy. It became apparent that privation, hardship and heavy fighting lay ahead. Hawaii was a training ground and spring board from which our armed forces moved on from one brilliant victory to another, climaxed finally with the capitulation and occupation of Japan. In the meantime members of our armed forces were having their pictures taken.

Men do not, as a rule, like to have their pictures taken. Only the few who take pride in their personal appearance and who have a keen desire to record that appearance, visit the photographer. But immediately following the blitz of December 7, 1941, Honolulu photographers, most of whom had previously devoted their attention to photographing women and children, landscape photography, or commercial work, found their establishments overrun with service men. These men did not want to have their pictures made but they had been urged, nagged, begged or bullied by their home folks until they submitted. Generally, they came because they wanted to make good their promise to either a wife, mother, girlfriend or sweetheart, who may have felt keenly the possibility that their man might never return. Some came willingly to show new uniforms, new ratings, or in a few instances because they really enjoyed being photographed. But most came reluctantly, grudgingly, unwillingly, in an unhappy mood. The situation taxed the ingenuity of the cameraman to overcome the psychological resistance and produce happy, natural likenesses of the subjects.

cont'd on p. 82

United States Army

Overseas

Write Message Here

Bolster the Line with Liberty Bonds

Soldier's Mail
Free
st Card
For Address Only
POST CARD
ADDRESS
CORRESPONDENCE

Occasionally the wife, fiancee or girlfriend came along, but quite early the servicemen's wives and families were evacuated to the mainland and the few who remained had war jobs. Most of the servicemen had left relatives, friends and families behind on the mainland.

No attempt is here made to record any of the facts about these men. They came from all parts of our country, from Maine to California, from Minnesota to Texas. They represented a wide variety of racial, occupational and educational backgrounds. There were New Yorkers, farmer boys from the Middle West, and miners from Montana and West Virginia.

This group of portraits has been selected at random from the thousands which were taken at this studio during the hectic days of the war. The contacts and associations with the subjects were almost entirely impersonal. Brevity was the keynote. Time did not afford asking questions, though occasionally a boy lingered long enough to tell the state from which he came and something of his former occupation. Not infrequently some boy later wrote from a forward base to ask that some trivial errand or mission be carried out—a service always warmly appreciated. The names are omitted; the subjects who sat for the pictures will remain anonymous. The burden of interest falls entirely upon the study of the faces themselves. The faces are adequate to reveal character, personality and temperament. May the pages be turned reverently, for undoubtedly there were some of the subjects who dedicated their all that the world might be a better place in which to live; from forward bases they will never return.

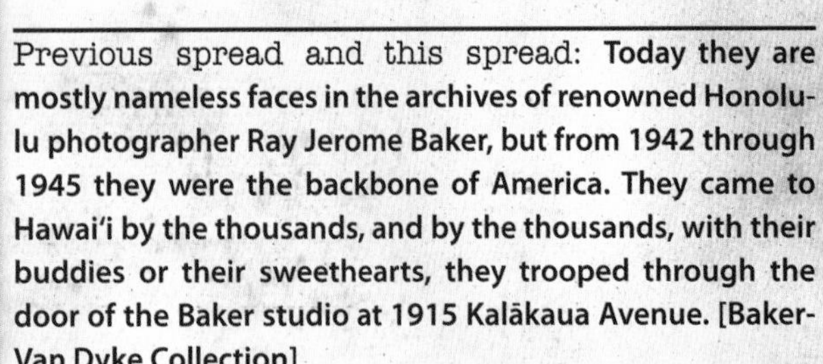

Previous spread and this spread: **Today they are mostly nameless faces in the archives of renowned Honolulu photographer Ray Jerome Baker, but from 1942 through 1945 they were the backbone of America. They came to Hawai'i by the thousands, and by the thousands, with their buddies or their sweethearts, they trooped through the door of the Baker studio at 1915 Kalākaua Avenue. [Baker-Van Dyke Collection]**

1. Recreation for enlisted men at the Royal Hawaiian Hotel, February 12, 1942. [*Honolulu Star-Bulletin*/University of Hawai'i War Records Depository/HWRD0632]

2. Hawai'i's world famous Royal Hawaiian hotel, mecca in the past years for famous tourists from all parts of the world, became a recreation center for the armed forces having been leased by the Navy. The $4,000,000 hotel, erected in 1926, ranked among the world's most colorful pleasure resorts. Sailors danced on the terrace with young USO hostesses, 1945. [*Honolulu Star-Bulletin*/ University of Hawai'i War Records Depository/HWRD0633]

3. United Service Organization (USO) Information Hut in front of the Army-Navy YMCA in Honolulu, 1942. [U.S. Army Signal Corps/University of Hawai'i War Records Depository/ HWRD1183]

4. To improve the morale of soldiers, the Army posted swing-era musician and singer Corporal Jim Cassel (second from left) at Fort DeRussey's Maluhia Enlisted Men's Club. Jim earlier found national acclaim by winning a Major Bowes radio competition aired from Radio City Music Hall. He signed up in the wake of the Pearl Harbor attack. At Fort DeRussey Jim played trombone and sang top pop hits at nightly dances.

Sailing on a mainland-bound post-war troopship Jim vowed to himself he would return to Hawai'i. He re-enrolled at Drake University to finish his music education degree. In 1951, forgoing a promising mainland musical career, he moved to Kaua'i with his Iowa bride Ruth to teach music at Waimea High. He also served as choir director at the historic Waimea U.C.C. church for 56 years. [Cassel family]

1. The United Service Organization (USO) lū'au in honor of Army, Navy and Red Cross nurses, given at the Hindrichson Estate in Wahiawā, October 11, 1942. [U.S. Army Signal Corps/ University of Hawai'i War Records Depository/HWRD1181]

2. Outside a curio shop, soldiers found an ancient poi-pounding board and J. Logan demonstrated the method and rhythm that went into the handling of the pounders hewn from lava rock. Left to right: Private John Slanina, J. Logan, owner of the shop, Sergeant Walter H. Roger, Corporal Andrew Faleshock, and Private First Class Gilbert Detter, July 11, 1943. [U.S. Army Signal Corps/University of Hawai'i War Records Depository/ HWRD1130]

3. Crowded dance floor of Maluhia, service men's recreation center at Fort DeRussy, opening day, May 1, 1943. [U.S. Army Signal Corps/University of Hawai'i War Records Depository/ HWRD1120]

4. A soldier entering the Army Bath Houses in Waikīkī, 1943. [U.S. Army Signal Corps/University of Hawai'i War Records Depository/HWRD1122]

5. Fort De Russy Recreational Center, 1942. [*Honolulu Star-Bulletin*/University of Hawai'i War Records Depository/HWRD0581]

V-J DAY

Civilians and military personnel alike received the news of Japan's surrender with wild jubilation. Within minutes, over 50,000 phone calls were made on O'ahu as friends and family spread the news. [National Archives]

People in Hawai'i reacted with little fanfare to the mass celebration of V-E Day in New York City and across the mainland in May 1945. War work went right on, and war workers criticized the mainland for its wild celebrations, for they saw the war was far from over for Hawai'i. To the war-weary Islands, the end of the distant European Theater hostilities meant the battle against Japan in the Pacific Theater would intensify, with countless more lives to be lost before final victory.

Martial law had been lifted in October 1944, but nightly blackouts and curfews continued through the summer of 1945.

Hawai'i held its breath waiting for news of Japan's surrender after the dropping of atomic bombs incinerated Japanese cities: Hiroshima on August 6, 1945, and four days later Nagasaki.

On V-J Day—August 14, 1945—word came at 1:42 p. m. that Allied forces were "victorious in the air, on the land and over the seas." The emperor of Japan had capitulated. The Pacific War was over. People went wild with joy across Hawai'i. To celebrate the arrival of peace, bells tolled, car horns blared, kids beat on pots and pans and garbage cans, air raid sirens wailed. In Honolulu within minutes, Bishop Street and downtown streets were covered in a torrent of confetti, in part made up of the volumes of government forms that had been regulating island life. Overcrowded military and civilian trucks, cars, and jeeps drove up and down Kalākaua Avenue in Waikīkī, large American flags waving, passengers, locals, and military barely hanging on. Crowds cheered V-J Day long into the night.

Victory Over Japan Day was officially celebrated on O'ahu on September 2, with a V-J Day Parade down Beretania Avenue.

With the war finally over, Hawai'i's citizens looked toward the future with a spirit of endless possibilities. ■

1. Civilians and service personnel rejoice together at the surrender of Japan to allied forces, 1945. [U.S. Army Signal Corps/University of Hawai'i War Records Depository/HWRD1374]

2. Pedestrians read V-E Day news on a street corner in Waikīkī, May 8, 1945. [*Honolulu Star-Bulletin*/University of Hawai'i War Records Depository/HWRD0747]

3. Soldiers and sailors crowded aboard a truck headed for downtown Honolulu via King Street, jubilantly hail Japan's acceptance of the Potsdam Ultimatum and the end of the war. August 1945. [U.S. Army Signal Corps/University of Hawai'i War Records Depository/HWRD1392]

MOVIES AND BOOKS

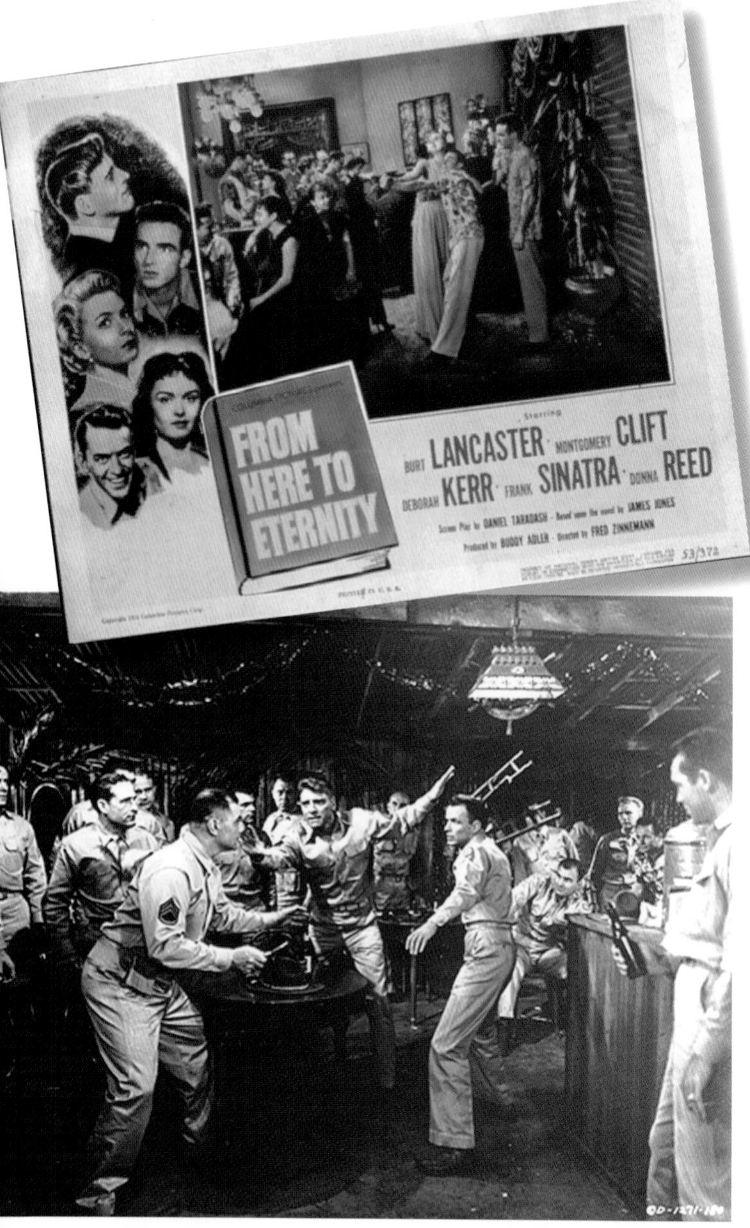

The military presence in Hawai'i was heightened during World War II, when more than a million servicemen passed through the Islands, and nearly one third of O'ahu was taken over by Army and Navy personnel. For over three years residents coped with blackouts, food control, fingerprinting, mail censorship, gas-mask and air raid drills, and martial law. Hollywood captured the spirit of Hawai'i at war in the Academy Award-winning film *From Here to Eternity,* the classic 1954 adaptation of the James Jones novel, starring Ernest Borgnine as "Fats," Burt Lancaster as "Sergeant Warden," and Frank Sinatra as "Maggio." [Luis Reyes Collection/Screen Gems]

The Pearl Harbor attack on December 7, 1941 served as a key scene in the plots of many Hollywood films.

Multiple-Oscar-winning 1953 drama *From Here to Eternity,* based on James Jones's best-selling literary World War II book of the same name, tells the gritty story of Army soldiers stationed at Schofield Barracks in the months leading up to Pearl Harbor. The passionate kiss by Burt Lancaster and Deborah Kerr rolling in the shorebreak of a Windward O'ahu cove is an iconic Hollywood scene. Frank Sinatra, playing Private Maggio, won the Best Supporting Actor award, helping the singer to revive his then-fading career.

Tora! Tora! Tora! from 1970 is a big-budget docudrama that shows the Pearl Harbor attack from the perspective of both the United States and Japan. Reenactments of key moments of the attack are portrayed using period aircraft and ships. Released during the hey days of rural plantation movie theaters, the audience gave the film a standing ovation at the Hale'iwa Theater when some of the few American fighter planes able to take off launched from nearby Hale'iwa Field.

In Harm's Way, director Otto Preminger's epic war film, is set in Hawai'i in the days surrounding the Pearl Harbor attack. The 1965 black-and-white film stars John Wayne and Kirk Douglas. It tells the story of U.S. Navy officers and their wives and lovers as World War II unfolds in the Islands.

Arguably the best Hollywood re-creations of air and sea scenes of the Pearl Harbor attack highlight director Michael Bay's 2001 film, *Pearl Harbor.* A love triangle unfolds, entangling two young Midwest men and a Pearl Harbor nurse.

The wartime-made *Remember Pearl Harbor* drama from 1942 (filmed in California) offers a Frank Capra–style patriotic take on how the Pearl Harbor attack rallied Americans into a global war.

Midway, released in 1976 and starring Charlton Heston, is a dramatic, fictionalized account of the U.S. Navy's historic defeat of a Japanese carrier fleet sent to

invade Midway Atoll as a stepping-stone to conquering Hawai'i. Watch scenes of the Navy's heroic dive-bombing runs that sank Japanese carriers and turned the tide of the Pacific War in a fateful battle against a superior force.

Gregory Peck plays Gen. Douglas MacArthur in the 1977 film, *MacArthur*. Featured is a Pearl Harbor meeting scene and the general signing the peace treaty with Japan aboard the battleship USS *Missouri*. Footage features the actual battleship as it was years prior to being sent to Pearl Harbor for permanent display.

The bombing of Pearl Harbor is a turning point in the romantic noir drama, *The Revolt of Mamie Stover*, starring Jane Russell. The movie portrays the life of a San Francisco prostitute who runs away from the law

1. The second assault on "battleship row" took place during the filming of *Tora! Tora! Tora!* on location where it actually happened over the Ford Island Naval Base at Pearl Harbor. [Luis Reyes Collection]

2. John Wayne as Admiral Rockwell Torrey and Patricia Neal as Lt. Maggie Haynes in *In Harm's Way*. [Luis Reyes Collection]

3. During a Civilian Defense Air Raid Test in which downtown Honolulu was evacuated, crowds of people pass Princess Theater, as they make their way up Fort Street. Notice the theater sign *Flight for Freedom*. [U.S. Army Signal Corps/University of Hawai'i War Records Depository]

1. General MacArthur, played by Gregory Peck, adds his signature to history at the Japanese surrender aboard the battleship USS *Missouri*. This scene from the movie *MacArthur* was filmed on the actual deck of the historic ship where the surrender took place. The USS *Missouri* is now permanently anchored at Pearl Harbor. [Luis Reyes Collection]

2. Jane Russell played Mamie Stover in this screen adaptation of William Bradford Huie's popular novel, *The Revolt of Mamie Stover*. [Luis Reyes Collection]

to Honolulu just prior to the Pearl Harbor attack. There she is torn between a romance with a successful writer and life in the underworld of Honolulu's Hotel Street.

Go For Broke, starring Van Johnson, is the 1951 drama that portrays the story of the highly decorated 442nd Regimental Combat Team composed of Americans of Japanese Ancestry. The film, in a rare positive World War II portrayal of Asian Americans, follows the Nisei AJA men from enlistment and basic training to the World War II battlefields in Italy and France. A number of documentaries detail the story of Hawai'i men serving in the 442nd, its predecessor the 100th infantry battalion, and the Military Intelligence Service, including *Beyond Barbed Wire,* documented by *Happy Days* actor Pat Morita.

Through telling the story of U.S. Navy sailors stationed on a faraway Pacific Island near the mythical isle of Bali Hai, the Academy Award–nominated 1958 film *South Pacific* captures the beauty of Hawai'i with a World War II theme. Filmed on Kaua'i and based on the hit Rogers & Hammerstein Broadway play of the same name, *South Pacific* offers an idealistic look at American servicemen stationed in an island paradise.

A trio of Kaua'i-made Hollywood feature films tell World War II stories set in South Pacific islands. Tony Curtis plays a Marine making a fateful crossing of a South Pacific Island in *Beachhead,* released in 1952; Ricky Nelson and Jack Lemmon star in the comic action film, *The Wackiest Ship in the Army;* and Frank Sinatra joined forces with Japanese filmmakers in producing and directing the antiwar-themed *None But the Brave* in 1965.

Portrayals of the early 1890s Royal Guard troops of the Kingdom of Hawai'i being threatened by Marines during the 1893 overthrow of the Hawaiian Kingdom highlight the 1970 film, *The Hawaiians.* The film is a follow-up to the successful movie version of author James Michener's blockbuster book, *Hawaii.* In *Princess Kaiulani,* from 2009, the royal troops are pictured, along with local militia, in the unsuccessful counterrevolution of 1895, as well as Hawai'i's Provisional Government troops from the same era. ■

1. The cast of *Pearl,* a multipart, five-hour television drama which aired in the 1970s by Stirling Silliphant: Angie Dickinson, Dennis Weaver, Lesley Ann Warren and Robert Wagner. *Pearl* is the explosive story of men and women living in the peacetime paradise of Hawai'i in 1941. Their lives are suddenly shattered on a quiet December morning when a Japanese attack from the skies ends the innocence of a nation.

2. Mitzi Gaynor as the U.S. nurse Nellie Forbush and Italian screen idol Rossano Brazzi as the French planter Emile DeBecque. In this scene from *South Pacific,* they are at his plantation located at a Promontory near Hanalei Bay, Kaua'i. [Twentieth Century Fox]

During World War II, four 155-milimeter guns were positioned at Panama Mount on the southeast rim of Punchbowl's crater. The guns had been removed by the time the above photo was taken in 1946. [U.S. Army Museum of Hawai'i]

POST WAR
HAWAI'I

RETURN OF THE 442ND REGIMENT

The 442nd Regimental Combat Team returned with great honor from the battlefields of Europe. About two-thirds of the regiment, almost all composed of Americans of Japanese Ancestry (AJAs), enlisted in Hawai'i; the remainder came mostly from California.

By the end of World War II, the 442nd, known as the "Purple Heart Battalion," was the most decorated unit for its size and length of service in the entire history of the U.S. armed forces. Replacements were made about 3.5 times for each of the 4,000 men who initially enlisted in April 1943. Some 14,000 Nisei (second-generation) men served all together in the unit, which became known for its "Go for Broke" rallying cry, a pidgin-English term from Hawai'i. They earned 9,486 Purple Hearts, twenty-one Medals of Honor, and a remarkable eight Presidential Unit Citations. More than 600 men were killed in combat,

The bravery of the 442nd and 100th in the European Theater, and the AJA men serving in the Military Intelligence Service in the Pacific Theater, improved life for all Americans of Japanese Ancestry. Their battle record and selfless sacrifices in combat turned around the sometimes negative attitude of Americans toward the Japanese in the United States and helped win early release for the 120,000 AJAs placed in internment camps following the Pearl Harbor attack.

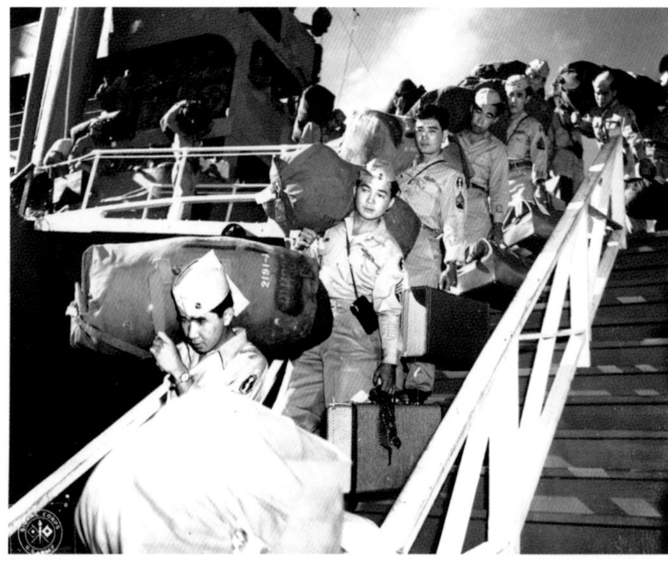

Members of the 442nd Regimental Combat Team make their way down the gangplank of the transport *Waterbury Victory* shortly after it docked in Honolulu on August 9, 1946. [U.S. Army Signal Corps/University of Hawai'i War Records Depository/HWRD1478]

On July 4, 1946, the men of the 442nd sailed into New York harbor aboard the SS *Wilson Victory* and were greeted by cheering crowds. In further recognition of their valor, eleven days later a reception was held for them in Washington, D.C. There President Harry Truman pinned the Presidential Unit Citation on the 442nd Regimental Combat Team colors. Truman remarked, "You fought not only the enemy, but you fought prejudice—and you have won." The 442nd was deactivated in Honolulu in 1946. While overseas, where their strong camaraderie grew in battle, there was talk among the 442nd men of gathering together in an organization once back home. By late December 1945, while the 442nd was still on occupation duty in Italy, men who had been already mustered out held a formal meeting in Honolulu to organize a postwar 442nd veterans' club in Hawai'i.

In July 1949, the first burials of men from the 442nd and the 100th Infantry Battalion killed in action during World War II were held at the National Memorial Cemetery of the Pacific at Punchbowl Crater.

The 442nd was reactivated in 1947 in the U.S. Army Reserve. The unit was mobilized in 1968 during the Vietnam War. Today the battalion is again in the U.S. Army Reserve, with headquarters at Fort Shafter, O'ahu.

In the decades following their return to Hawai'i, men of the 442nd found success in the Islands and led the way in electing a wave of Democrats who reformed

1. For many islanders, the return to civilian life was gradual, as the military slowly released its volunteer soldiers. In August of 1946, Sgt. Shige Fukuda of the 442nd Regimental Combat Team and his girlfriend, Edna Oda, read his discharge paper after a Kapi'olani Park Veterans Day Parade. In the postwar years, many young Nisei veterans took advantage of the GI Bill to pursue a college education on the mainland. [U.S. Army Signal Corps/University of Hawai'i War Records Depository/HWRD1488]

2. Lieutenant Unkei Uchima of Kaua'i of the 442nd Regimental Combat Team is presented with a lei from a hula dancer aboard the transport *Waterbury Victory* upon its entrance into the Honolulu Harbor on August 9, 1946. [U.S. Army Signal Corps/University of Hawai'i War Records Depository/HWRD1487]

3. Members of the 442nd Regimental Combat Team, veterans of the Italian and European campaigns, prepare to debark from their transport, the *Waterbury Victory,* in Honolulu Harbor after a long journey from New York, 1946. [U.S. Army Signal Corps/University of Hawai'i War Records Depository/HWrD1483]

politics in Hawai'i. Daniel Inouye, originally classified 4-C (enemy alien) during the war, became a prominent senator representing Hawai'i in Congress for decades. Sparky Matsunaga of Kaua'i was elected to the House of Representatives. Other 442nd veterans became prominent in business, education, and other professional fields.

In 2000, after fifty-five years, twenty members of the 442nd, including Sen. Daniel Inouye, were awarded the Medal of Honor by President Bill Clinton. Immediately following World War II, only one Medal of Honor was awarded to an AJA soldier. Private First Class Sadao S. Nunemori of the 100th Infantry Battalion, 442nd, from Los Angeles received the posthumous award. ■

PUNCHBOWL CEMETERY

Aerial view with Punchbowl in the foreground, Diamond Head in the background and Honolulu and Waikīkī in between. [Douglas Peebles]

National Memorial Cemetery of the Pacific

The National Memorial Cemetery of the Pacific is a solemn place of honor set above the flow of life in busy Honolulu. Buried and remembered there are thousands of men and women of the armed forces of the United States who gave their lives while serving their nation, as well as those who served in the military. The cemetery is administered by the National Cemetery Association of the U.S. Department of Veterans Affairs and serves together with the American Military Cemetery in Manila as America's national cemeteries located in the Pacific.

About 53,000 veterans and their dependents are buried here or have their ashes interred, including veterans of World War I, World War II, the Korean War, and the Vietnam War, including some 700 burials of those killed in the Pearl Harbor attack.

Commonly known as Punchbowl Cemetery, the memorial is a 112-acre field of green lawns containing concentric circles of grave markers and banyan-tree lined walkways. The granite grave markers are set ground level, unlike the distinct white crosses and Star of David markers found at Normandy Beach and other national cemeteries.

Punchbowl Cemetery is located inside an extinct volcanic crater known in ancient Hawai'i as Pūowaina and nicknamed Punchbowl in the early 1800s for its *round* shape.

Five million people visit the cemetery each year. Admission is free, a visitor center is located at the entrance, and a touring time of at least one hour is recommended. Parking is available in back of and to the side of the Honolulu Memorial near the cemetery entrance.

Visitors come to pay their respects to those interred and to take in the panoramic views of Diamond Head and the south shore of O'ahu visible from the crater's rim. On weekends, volunteer veterans serve as guides. Visitors are welcome to roam among the graves and there are benches available to sit on.

Ship masts greet visitors who proceed to the Honolulu Memorial, which honors the war dead from World War II, the Korean War, and the Vietnam War. It is located against the wall of the bowl-shaped inner crater. The American Battle Monuments Commission dedicated the Honolulu Memorial in 1966. In its ten "Courts of the Missing" are inscribed the names of 28,778 soldiers and sailors missing in action or buried at sea in the Pacific during World War II (except those named at the Manila cemetery), the Korean War, and the Vietnam War. The names are listed alphabetically and by service name. Names of Medal of Honor winners are noted with stars and their names are inscribed in gold leaf.

A thirty-foot statue of Columbia, female personification of the United States, is emblazoned on the tower of the chapel at the monument. Of interest especially to military history buffs are two galleries displaying oversize colorful and informative maps of major Pacific World War II theaters of combat and battles such as Pearl Harbor, Midway, and Iwo Jima.

At the bottom of the steps of the Honolulu Memorial is a memorial pathway where sixty descriptive

Pūowaina

Pūowaina is the Hawaiian place name of Punchbowl Crater, meaning "Hill of Sacrifice." Human sacrifices to Hawaiian gods were made at an altar located at the crater in the days of ancient Hawai'i.

The crater is the former site of a nineteenth-century Hawaiian fort where cannons were mounted by Kamehameha to signal the arrival of ships. In the mid-1800s, the community Christmas celebration in Honolulu featured a large vat of flaming oil spilling down the face of the crater, simulating a volcanic eruption.

As the homes and businesses of downtown Honolulu spread out beginning in the 1880s, leasehold lands on the slope of Punchbowl Crater were developed. The Hawai'i National Guard employed the crater as a rifle range in the 1930s prior to the Pearl Harbor attack in 1941. Several years after the attack, shore batteries were placed on the rim of the crater in defense of Pearl Harbor and Honolulu Harbor.

The first proposal to place a cemetery within Punchbowl Crater came in the 1890s, but it was rejected owing to fear of polluting city water.

In 1943, the governor of the Territory of Hawai'i offered the site for a national cemetery. The offer was acceptable to the U.S. War Department, and the land was donated. The project moved forward in 1948, with a great need to move the remains of thousands of World War II servicemen from a cemetery in Guam. Congress appropriated the funds for Punchbowl Crater, and construction began.

The remains of servicemen returned from Pacific Theater war sites, including Japanese POW camps, were the first burials. Graves were marked with white wooden crosses and Stars of David, mirroring American war cemeteries in Europe and Asia.

The first interment was made on Jan. 4, 1949, and the National Memorial Cemetery of the Pacific opened to the public on July 19, 1949. A ceremony was held for an unknown soldier, two Marines, an Army officer, and more notably Ernie Pyle, the nationally known roving World War II correspondent who was killed during the Battle of Okinawa. The dedication was held on the fourth anniversary of V-J Day on September 2, 1949. Graves for the remains of over 13,000 World War II soldiers and sailors are now at Punchbowl Cemetery. Flat granite markers later replaced the white crosses and Stars of David.

1

2

1. An Army honor guard stands at attention at the National Memorial of the Pacific. [Archives of the National Memorial Cemetery of the Pacific]

2. Solemn lines of caskets await burial on January 5, 1949. [Archives of the National Memorial Cemetery of the Pacific]

markers have been placed by veterans organizations and governments honoring specific groups such as the 442nd Regimental Combat Team. Residents of Hawaiʻi who served in the Civil War from 1861 to 1865 are now honored with a bronze and stone memorial dedicated by the Hawaiʻi Sons of the Civil War Memorial Committee.

The National Memorial Cemetery of the Pacific has space available for cremated remains of eligible veterans. Casketed remains can sometimes be placed in the same gravesite of previously interred family members. Periodically burial space becomes available due to disinterment from an existing gravesite. ■

1. **Flag-draped World War II caskets are escorted by men of the U.S. Army including Hawai'i veterans.[Archives of the National Memorial Cemetery of the Pacific]**

2. **Nearly 500 of the dead from Pearl Harbor were temporarily interred at Nu'uanu O'ahu Cemetery during the January 1, 1942 memorial service for the fallen servicemen. [National Archives and Records Administration]**

3, 4. **Once the scene of sacrifices, Punchbowl became a destination for Christian groups who flocked to the Easter Sunrise service held there each year, as did this group on March 23, 1940. [U.S. Army Museum of Hawai'i]**

Visiting The National Memorial Cemetery of the Pacific

The National Memorial Cemetery of the Pacific is located inside Punchbowl Crater, which is located ma uka (inland) of the H-1 Freeway, above central Honolulu, about midway between Waikīkī and Honolulu International Airport. To drive to the cemetery, take exit 21A or 21B off the H-1 Freeway and follow signs. Another route is taking Ward Avenue ma uka off Ala Moana Blvd. and making a right at Prospect Street and follow the signs into Punchbowl. Or look for signs along the Honolulu end of the Pali Highway, ma uka of the H-1 Freeway.

It is possible to reach zPunchbowl Cemetery riding TheBus, but this requires an uphill walk from the bus stop. Go to www.thebus.org for route information.

Visitation Hours:

- The cemetery is open seven days a week.
- Sept. 30 thru March 1, from 8:00 a.m. until 5:30 p.m.
- March 2 thru Sept. 29, from 8:00 a.m. until 6:30 p.m.
- On Memorial Day, the cemetery is open from 7:00 a.m. until 7:00 p.m.

Cemetery phone number:
(808) 532-3720

1. **Service members, veterans and Hawai'i's residents participate in the 66th Mayor's Memorial Day Ceremony at the National Memorial Cemetery of the Pacific at Punchbowl, May 25, 2015. [U.S. Navy photo by Mass Communication Specialist 2nd Class Laurie Dexter]**

2. **Two lei rest on a the plaque of a U.S. service member during the Veterans Day ceremony on November 11, 2012. [U.S. Navy photo by Mass Communication Specialist Seaman Diana Quinlan]**

3. **Anzac Day remembrance at the National Memorial Cemetery of the Pacific, Honolulu on April 25, 2015, in honor and commemoration of the soldiers who sacrificed their lives on the Gallipoli Peninsula, Turkey in 1915. [U.S. Navy photo by Mass Communication Specialist 1st Class Jay M. Chu]**

1. The joint service color guard performs the march of the colors during the Prisoner of War and Missing in Action Recognition Day Ceremony, September 18, 2015. [U.S. Marine Corps photo by Lance Cpl. Jonathan E. Lopez Cruet]

2. An Honor Guard holds their rifles at port arms, prior to a three-volley salute during the Mayor's Memorial Day Ceremony, May 25, 2015. [U.S. Marine Corps photo by Cpl. Erik Estrada]

3. Chris Farley, U.S. Navy veteran and National Memorial Cemetery of the Pacific (NMCP) caretaker, reads names of fallen service members, November 28, 2015. Farley is a U.S. Navy veteran who served from 1982 to 1987 as an air traffic controller. He is responsible for the maintenance of the 112.5 acres of land that make up the cemetery, the 56,971 gravesites of those who are interred in-ground or in-columbarium, and the 28,788 fallen who are memorialized in the courts of the missing. [U.S. Air Force photo by Staff Sgt. Christopher Hubenthal]

4. Veterans line up to participate in an official wreath presentation during the Veterans Day ceremony on November 11, 2012. [U.S. Navy photo by Mass Communication Specialist Seaman Diana Quinlan]

WORLD WAR II VALOR IN THE PACIFIC NATIONAL MONUMENT

The entrance to the World War II Valor in the Pacific National Monument which includes the USS *Arizona* Memorial, USS *Oklahoma* Memorial, and USS *Utah* Memorial. [Douglas Peebles]

The Pearl Harbor–Ford Island Memorials

In 1950, Pacific Fleet Commander Admiral Arthur Radford began a tradition of raising and lowering an American flag flying from a flagpole hoisted to the main mast of the sunken hulk of the USS *Arizona.* From this simple and poignant beginning, a temporary memorial was placed amidships over the remains of the battleship's deckhouse. It wasn't until 1955, due to Defense Department budget constraints, that a large basalt memorial stone and plaque were placed over the deckhouse. Beginning in 1958, extensive fundraising efforts were undertaken and financial support from Congress was sought to pay for the construction of a formal memorial. Fundraising events included a concert at Bloch Arena at Pearl Harbor starring Elvis Presley from which every dollar raised went to the USS *Arizona* Memorial fund. On Memorial Day 1962, a dedication ceremony opened the landmark memorial, with its white, 182-foot-long, 200-person capacity structure that still stands today.

The USS *Arizona* Memorial soon drew crowds of visitors who boarded a Navy launch from a dock moored next to a parking lot along Kamehameha Highway at Pearl Harbor. In 1980, the U.S. National Park Service joined forces with the Navy in providing a more in-depth experience for the thousands of visitors who went on the tour each day.

Today the USS *Arizona* Memorial is the centerpiece of the National Park Service's World War II Valor in the Pacific National Monument at Pearl Harbor. The boat launch ride to the USS *Arizona* Memorial is now just one

This display of plaques located on the grounds of the USS *Arizona* Memorial Visitor Center lists the names of all the casualties United States forces suffered during the attack on Pearl Harbor.[Douglas Peebles]

segment of a visitor destination experience that encompasses four distinct World War II era memorials located at Pearl Harbor and Ford Island, in a project coordinated through the Pearl Harbor Historic Partners organization. With four attractions now open, the length of a visit can comfortably extend to two days or longer compared to the relatively short ride out and back to the USS *Arizona* Memorial visitors of past years enjoyed.

The gateway to the World War II Valor in the Pacific National Monument is located at the Pearl Harbor Visitor Center, located along Kamehameha Highway near Aloha Stadium. What was once a parking lot with a small building and a maze of rope barriers to line up visitors boarding the boat launch has become a multimedia experience and a complex of visitor attractions and services.

The twenty-minute-or-so boat launch ride to the USS *Arizona* Memorial is now the final phase of a seventy-five-minute tour featuring a theater and film dedicated to telling the story of the December 7, 1941, attack.

And at the Pearl Harbor Visitor Center, tickets and transportation are available to three other major memorial sites.

The World War II–era USS *Bowfin* submarine is restored and moored at the Pearl Harbor Visitor Center and within walking distance of the USS *Arizona* Memorial buildings. An admission ticket separate from the USS *Arizona* Memorial tour provides access to a walk-through tour of the tight quarters and battle stations inside the restored submarine. The ticket also includes a visit to the Pacific Submarine Museum, which displays the history of the U.S. Submarine Service in the Pacific.

The third site is the massive battleship USS *Missouri,* moored in 1999 adjacent to the USS *Arizona* Memorial. A tour is offered of the decks and interior workings of the last battleship active in the U.S. Navy, and the ship where the peace treaty with Imperial Japan was signed in Tokyo Harbor in 1945. Visitors going on a USS *Missouri* tour are transported from the Pearl Harbor Visitor Center aboard a shuttle bus to the pier on Ford Island where the USS *Missouri* is moored. There is a separate admission for the variety of USS *Missouri* tours available.

The fourth site is a center of military aviation history and the newest attraction: the Pacific Aviation Museum Pearl Harbor. The Pacific Aviation Museum is located on Ford Island and occupies Hangers 37 and 79 and the Ford Island Control Tower. All three were in use by American armed forces aviators during the attack on Pearl Harbor. Exhibits of significant restored World War II–era aircraft highlight the museum tour. The museum was organized when a group of local residents approached the Navy with plans to create a world-class aviation museum using surplus World War II-era hangers located on Ford Island. This plan fit perfectly with the Navy's goals for use of the land drawn up in consultation with the Historic Hawai'i Foundation and the National Trust for Historic Preservation. Transportation is provided aboard a shuttle bus that leaves from the Pearl Harbor Visitor Center. ■

THE USS *ARIZONA* MEMORIAL

The USS *Arizona* Memorial as seen from the water. The Tree of Life is represented in the smaller windows to the far right. [Douglas Peebles]

The distinctive, white-walled USS *Arizona* Memorial floating in the East Loch of Pearl Harbor symbolizes America's remembrance of the Pearl Harbor attack of December 7, 1941. The somber memorial straddles the sunken hull of the battleship USS *Arizona*. Within the hull lie the remains of hundreds of its officers and crewmen.

There is only one way for the public to tour the USS *Arizona* Memorial, and that is aboard a Navy shuttle boat. Access to the tour is through the USS *Arizona* Memorial Visitor Center, which opened in 1980 and is operated by the National Park Service. The Pearl Harbor site is part of the National Park Service's World War II Valor in the Pacific National Monument network of interpreted sites located across the Pacific Basin.

The Pearl Harbor Visitor Center is also the primary entrance for visitors coming to Pearl Harbor and Ford Island to tour the USS *Arizona* Memorial and the USS *Bowfin* submarine at the visitor center, as well as the major World War-II-related sites on nearby Ford Island—the USS *Missouri* and the Pacific Aviation Museum.

Ticket pickup and orientation facilities are located at the visitor center.

The Pearl Harbor–Ford Island monument and memorial complex ranks among the top three most heavily visited tourist destinations in Hawai'i. There are daily crowds, but the busiest seasons are summer, winter holidays, and spring break. Daily visitor counts often top 4,000.

Tickets to the USS *Arizona* Memorial tour are sold according to tour times and to guarantee a ticket, it should be purchased well in advance. Tours last seventy-five minutes, hold 150 people, and begin at fifteen-minute intervals, the first at 8:00 a.m. and the last at

1. **Ferry boats using clean fuel technology shuttle more than 1.5 million passengers a year to the USS *Arizona* Memorial. [U.S. Navy photo by Mass Communication Specialist 2nd Class Daniel Barker]**

2. **U.S. sailors from the Joint Base Pearl Harbor-Hickam Ceremonial Guard place a wreath presented by survivor Lauren Bruner in the shrine room at the USS *Arizona* Memorial on June 6, 2013. [U.S. Navy photo by Mass Communication Specialist 2nd Class Tiarra Fulgham]**

3:00 p.m. daily. The weather at Pearl Harbor, located in leeward O'ahu, is usually sunny with light trade winds.

The Aloha Court is located at the entrance to the visitor center. Here visitors receive information about planning their day at Pearl Harbor, and this is where tickets are available and information about what to do and what to see at Pearl Harbor.

Two exhibit galleries—"Road to War" and "Attack"—provide a background on the Pearl Harbor attack on O'ahu and what it led to. Displays feature memorabilia, photographs, artifacts from the battle, and other exhibits. Recorded accounts of eyewitnesses to the attack can be played at conveniently located kiosks.

Located throughout the visitor center are interpretive wayside exhibits. Features include a historic photo of Pearl Harbor as it was in 1941 superimposed across a panorama of the Navy port as it is today.

Adjacent to the exhibit galleries is the Pearl Harbor Memorial Theater. Here visitors begin their seventy-five-minute USS *Arizona* Memorial tour program. It begins with a viewing of a twenty-three-minute documentary film on the December 7, 1941 attack. Following the viewing, visitors proceed to a dock where they board a Navy-run shuttle boat launch for a short ride that crosses the calm waters of the East Loch over to the USS *Arizona* Memorial, located just offshore of Ford Island.

Arriving at the USS *Arizona* Memorial, visitors step off the launch and walk to the Entry Room, where flags are displayed from the eight states represented by the eight battleships moored at Pearl Harbor the day of the attack, plus one for the USS *Utah*, which was a target ship. There is a tradition of bringing along a flower lei to toss in the harbor as a remembrance to the men who died aboard the battleship. Next they move on to the Assembly Room, where visitors may take a closer look at the silent hull of the USS *Arizona* as seen below in the clear water of Pearl Harbor. Shiny oil slicks float on the surface of the harbor, generated by tiny drops still leaking from the fuel bunkers of the USS *Arizona*. Finally, the Shrine Room contains a great marble wall where they read the names of the 1,177 sailors and Marines who perished aboard the USS *Arizona* the day of the attack. ■

3. Japanese soldiers and sailors render honors during a wreath-laying ceremony at the USS *Arizona* Memorial during a scheduled port visit on August 4, 2015. The ceremony was meant to pay respect to those who lost their lives during the attack on Pearl Harbor Dec. 7, 1941. [U.S. Navy photo by Mass Communication Specialist 2nd Class Johans Chavarro]

4. Sailors aboard the aircraft carrier USS T*heodore Roosevelt* render honors as the ship passes the USS *Arizona* Memorial, November 15, 2015. [U.S. Navy Photo by Mass Communication Specialist Seaman Chad M. Trudeau]

5. John Hughes, Pearl Harbor survivor, looks at the names displayed on the USS *Arizona* Memorial wall at the Pearl Harbor Day Commemoration Ceremony held on December 7, 2015. [U.S. Marine Corps photo by Cpl. Wesley Timm]

6. American and Japanese veterans pour bourbon whiskey into the hallowed waters of Pearl Harbor as a way to observe and celebrate the continued peace and reconciliation between the two nations during a Blackened Canteen ceremony as part of the Pearl Harbor Day—74th Commemoration Anniversary November 6, 2015. [U.S. Air Force photo by Staff Sgt. Christopher Hubenthal]

1. In honor of Memorial Day visitors to the World War II Valor in the Pacific National Monument participate in the National Park Service sunset tour of the USS *Arizona* Memorial, May 27, 2014. A Pacific Fleet Band bugler performed evening taps and Joint Base Pearl Harbor-Hickam Honors and Ceremonies flag detail performed evening colors on the memorial. [U.S. Navy photo by Mass Communication Specialist 1st Class Daniel Barker]

2. Participants attending the Pearl Harbor Day Commemoration Ceremony bow their heads during the benediction given on the USS *Arizona* Memorial, December 7, 2015. Civilians, veterans, and service members came together for the 74th anniversary to remember and give their respect to those who fought and lost their lives during the attack. [U.S. Marine Corps photo by Cpl. Wesley Timm]

3. Electronics Technician 3rd Class Timothy Crossno (left) and Cryptologic Technician Interpretive 3rd Class Adam Crist, assigned to Joint Base Pearl Harbor-Hickam Honors and Ceremonies flag detail, perform evening colors on the USS *Arizona* Memorial, May 27, 2014. [U.S. Navy photo by Mass Communication Specialist 1st Class Daniel Barker]

Pearl Harbor Visitor Center Info Box

- **Location:** The visitor center is located on the East Loch of Pearl Harbor, along Kamehameha Highway west of the Honolulu International Airport and east of Aloha Stadium. The visitor center is located outside of the Joint Base Pearl Harbor-Hickam. For online map searches, type in the address 1 Arizona Memorial Place, Honolulu HI 96818 to avoid mistaking the visitor center for the entrance to the Joint Base.
- Parking at the Pearl Harbor Visitor Center is free. Lots are located in front of the main entrance.
- No purses, handbags, backpacks, camera bags, diaper bags, or other items that offer concealment are allowed in the visitor center or on the USS *Arizona* Memorial tour.
- **Booking Tickets:** It is advisable to reserve your tickets to the USS *Arizona* Memorial well in advance of a visit. Go to www.recreation.gov to reserve tickets for tours of the USS *Arizona* Memorial and other Pearl Harbor Historic Sites. A one-day Passport to Pearl Harbor ticket allows access to the USS *Arizona* Memorial, the USS *Missouri*, the USS *Bowfin*, and the Pacific Aviation Museum. Reserved tickets can be picked up at the National Park Service's Ticket Desk at the Pearl Harbor Visitor Center. To take in all four sites requires about eight or nine hours. The visitor center opens at 7 a.m. and closes at 5 p.m.
- **Holiday Hours:** The Pearl Harbor Visitor Center is open daily from 7:00 a.m. to 4:30 p.m. and is closed Thanksgiving Day, December 25, and January 1.
- **Security Information:** Strict security measures prohibit purses, handbags, fanny packs, backpacks, camera bags, diaper bags, luggage and/or other items that offer concealment. Visitors may bring cameras, cell phones, and wallets, although since no bags are allowed, you are encouraged to pack lightly. A storage facility operated by the USS *Bowfin* Submarine Museum & Park is available in the immediate area of the entrance to the Pearl Harbor Visitor Center. There is a nominal storage fee of $3 per bag. The storage facility is in operation daily from 6:30 a.m. to 5:30 p.m.
- **USS *Oklahoma* and USS *Utah* memorials:** The USS *Oklahoma* Memorial and USS *Utah* Memorial on Ford Island are both open from dawn to dusk; however, unlike the USS *Oklahoma* Memorial, the USS *Utah* Memorial is not currently available to the public via shuttle. Access to the USS *Utah* Memorial is currently limited to visitors who have military base access.
- **Dress:** Civilian visitors are reminded that they are visiting a site where there was a tremendous loss of life during the attack on Pearl Harbor. Sandals are permissible, but bathing suits or profane T-shirts are discouraged. Military visitors are within the boundary of Joint Base Pearl Harbor-Hickam, and military regulations relating to dress are enforced by Navy personnel. Military visitors in uniform are required to dress in Class B or better in order to gain access to the shuttle boats to the USS *Arizona* Memorial. Battle dress uniform is not allowed on the USS *Arizona* Memorial, though it is allowed throughout the visitor center and at sites on Ford Island. Military visitors are welcome to wear civilian clothes when they visit.
- **Pets:** Pets are not permitted at the World War II Valor in the Pacific National Monument. Service animals are allowed.

Visitor Information Web Sites

- National Park Service, World War II Valor in the Pacific: www.nps.gov/valr/index.htm
- USS *Bowfin*: www.bowfin.org
- Pacific Aviation Museum, Pearl Harbor: www.pacificaviationmuseum.org
- USS *Missouri*: www.ussmissouri.org

THE USS *MISSOURI*

The USS *Missouri* stands guard over the USS *Arizona* Memorial in the waters of Pearl Harbor. [Douglas Peebles]

The USS *Missouri* (BB-63), the "Mighty Mo," is the World War II battleship best known for being the ship onboard which the Empire of Japan formally surrendered, ending World War II. The *Missouri*'s three-football-fields-long hull and superstructure are massive. Impressive are the ship's nine sixteen-inch guns, which are capable of firing with great accuracy a 2,700-pound projectile up to twenty-three miles.

The *Missouri* was the last battleship constructed by the United States in an era when the aircraft carrier superseded the battleship as the Navy's top combat ship. She was built at the Brooklyn Navy Yard and commissioned in June 1944. In Pacific Theater battles toward the end of the war, the USS *Missouri* fired its huge shells at enemy positions on Iwo Jima and Okinawa.

She served in the Korean War, was mothballed in 1955, and recommissioned in 1984 during a boost in naval power. She saw action again during Operation Desert Storm in 1991.

In 1998 she was donated to the USS *Missouri* Memorial Association and was towed to Pearl Harbor to be used as a floating museum, moored just 500 yards away from the USS *Arizona* Memorial. The USS *Missouri* opened as a museum in January 1999.

Sen. Daniel Inouye of Hawai'i assisted in having Hawai'i chosen as the final home port of the USS *Missouri,* thus bringing the battleship symbolic of the end of the Pacific War to the site where the war started. So as not to overshadow the USS *Arizona* Memorial, the bow of the USS *Missouri* faces it.

Battleship *Missouri* Tours are run by the USS *Missouri* Memorial Association. Ticketing for the tours is provided at the Pearl Harbor Visitor Center and online. *Missouri* visitors leave from the Pearl Harbor Visitor Center aboard a shuttle bus for the short ride across the

A bronze statue of Admiral Chester W. Nimitz stands a welcoming duty post at the entrance to the Battleship *Missouri* Memorial. [Douglas Peebles]

A four-inch, 50 caliber aft gun located on deck of the USS *Bowfin*.[Douglas Peebles]

Admiral Clarey Bridge to Ford Island, where the USS *Missouri* is berthed within the grounds of Naval Station Pearl Harbor. Only vehicles with a Navy base pass are allowed to drive onto Ford Island.

A ticket to the USS *Missouri* includes a complimentary optional thirty-five-minute guided walking tour of the ship's teak main decks that provides a good introduction to the ship. Docents aboard the battleship help answer questions and guide visitors.

The popular seventy-five-minute "Heart of the *Missouri*" tour provides up to ten visitors at a time, with a look at the mechanics that gave the battleship its great speed and firepower. The tour is for the mobile, for it requires climbing ten sets of tight, narrow stairs, low overheads, and stepping around other obstacles.

Sites of interest aboard include the aft (rear) deck, where the foreign minister of Japan signed the surrender papers facing General Douglas MacArthur. The Kamikaze Deck is where a Japanese Zero hit and damaged the battleship during the Battle of Okinawa. The view from the bridge of the USS *Missouri* offers a panoramic look at Pearl Harbor and the USS *Arizona* Memorial.

The tour goes below decks, too, for a look at living and dining quarters, a command center, and more. ■

1. Navy boys salute Foreign Minister Mamoru Shigemitsu, in top hat, as he prepares to step aboard. Marines watch in the foreground. [National Archives]

2. Foreign Minister Mamoru Shigemitsu, with cane, stands in the front row of the Japanese delegation. Beside him is General Yoshijiro Umezu of the Imperial General Staff. [National Archives]

3. Fleet Admiral Chester W. Nimitz signs the surrender papers. Behind him, from left, are General Douglas MacArthur, Admiral William F. Halsey, and Rear Admiral Frederick C. Sherman. [National Archives]

4. Director Joseph Sargent stages a reenactment of the Japanese surrender ceremony aboard the USS *Missouri* for the 1977 feature film, *MacArthur*. The ship was moved away from its pier at the Puget Sound Naval Shipyard for the filming. [Puget Sound Naval Shipyard]

5. This bronze plaque marks the location of the surrender table on deck. It was designed and cast by workers in the Norfolk Navy Yard. [National Archives]

THE USS *BOWFIN*

The USS *Bowfin* Submarine Museum and Park is located within the Pearl Harbor Visitor Center. A visit aboard the historic World War II submarine USS *Bowfin,* which is berthed alongside the museum, and into the museum itself, requires a ticket separate from the USS *Arizona* Memorial tour.

While the USS *Arizona* Memorial complex is operated with federal funds, the USS *Bowfin* exhibit is operated by a private nonprofit institution. Admission fees and gift shop sales contribute to the maintenance of the historic World War II submarine and the adjacent Pacific Submarine Museum.

The fleet attack submarine USS *Bowfin* (SS-287) was launched at the Portsmouth Naval Shipyard in Kittery, Maine, one year to the day following the attack on Pearl Harbor. The launching date led to the Balao-class submarine being nicknamed the "Pearl Harbor Avenger." During nine combat patrols in Japanese waters, the USS *Bowfin* sank thirty-eight ships and small craft. Downed American pilots who ejected in the Pacific were rescued by USS *Bowfin* crews, including President George H. W. Bush. She patrolled almost 100,000 nautical miles prior to her decommissioning in 1947.

Today visitors walk through the interior of the sub and see firsthand what life on board the cramped, diesel-powered USS *Bowfin* was like during World War II for the eighty-man crew. The preservation of the USS *Bowfin* and its submariner heritage is thanks to a dedicated organization of volunteers known as the Pacific Fleet Submarine Memorial Association (PFSMA). The group acquired the USS *Bowfin* from the U.S. Navy in 1979 and opened the sub for tours to the public in 1981. Today the Pacific Submarine Museum broadens the visitor's experience of the world of the Navy's World War II submarine service.

Before boarding the historic World War II submarine USS *Bowfin,* visitors are provided a digital audio player with narration of their tour. Numbers displayed inside the submarine correspond with audio track numbers on the players. The one-hour tour necessitates a walk through the tight quarters, ducking low through the narrow passageways located between compartments. The submarine tour is like stepping onto the set of a Hollywood submarine movie. Weaving through the obstacles provides a glimpse of what life below the sea was like aboard the sub, including the crew's stacked-bunk living quarters, the galley, torpedo room, the periscope and control center, and more.

The USS *Bowfin* Submarine, docked permanently at the WWII Valor in the Pacific National Monument. [Douglas Peebles]

The 10,000-square-foot Pacific Submarine Museum features exhibits of U.S. Submarine Service–related battle flags, photos, paintings, submarine recruiting posters, and weapon systems. Flags and models of the USS *Bowfin* portray the sub's nine Pacific war patrols, cruising between Australia and the Philippines and elsewhere. Exhibits include a rare display of a Poseidon C-3 missile with its electronics, hydraulics, and propulsion systems viewable; and a McCann Rescue Chamber such as that used in the only successful rescue of officers and crewmen from a sunken sub: the USS *Squalus* in 1939.

A waterfront memorial at the USS *Bowfin* Park section of the Pearl Harbor Visitor Center honors the fifty-two American submarines and the 3,500 submariners lost during World War II. Outdoor exhibits include a fifty-four-foot-long modified Imperial Japanese Navy Long Lance Torpedo, known in Japanese as a Kaiten, which was a manned torpedo designed for suicide missions. ■

PACIFIC AVIATION MUSEUM

The Pacific Aviation Museum Pearl Harbor, housed in historic hangars 37 and 79 adjacent to Ford Island's Luke Airfield, has a rotating display of planes large and small. [Douglas Peebles]

The Pacific Aviation Museum Pearl Harbor preserves the heritage of the fighters, bombers, PBYs, and other aircraft flown in the Pacific War. The aircraft museum is located inside two hangars on Ford Island that survived the Pearl Harbor attack. The museum is operated by a nonprofit board of directors, with former president George W. H. Bush serving as honorary chairman. Bush's actual naval training Stearman N2S-3 plane is on display.

The Pacific Aviation Museum's collection of key World War II planes is significant in the history of global warfare, for the meticulously restored and curated aircraft symbolize the major shift in naval warfare that resulted from the attack at Pearl Harbor on December 7, 1941. On that Day of Infamy, the fighters and bombers taking off from Imperial Japanese Navy aircraft a few hundred miles north of Oʻahu decimated the battleships of the U.S. Pacific Fleet. For the first time in a major military engagement, air power reigned supreme over naval forces.

The expertly restored vintage aircraft in the Pacific Aviation Museum are displayed along with interpretive signage, and some feature a diorama backdrop. While other air museums have many more planes on display, none are located at the site of a major historic battle, nor do they have buildings riddled with bullet holes in their walls and glass hangar windowpanes.

On a self-guided tour, visitors walk through Hangar 37 and the second phase of the museum in nearby Hangar 79, known as the Restoration Hangar. On the "Aviator's Tour," a volunteer docent interprets for visitors the displays of aircraft, providing a colorful commentary on the Pearl Harbor attack, Pacific War aviation history, and more.

Hangar 37 is a former 42,000-square-foot Navy seaplane hangar that survived the bombing of Pearl Harbor and is now used to tell the story of military aviation in the Pacific War from 1941 to through 1942. Entering the lobby, look down at the floor to see a mural of an aerial view of Pearl Harbor. The tour begins with a movie introduction. Visitors enter a 200-seat theater to view a twelve-minute film featuring historic footage of the attack on Pearl Harbor, then walk down a corridor that displays sights and sounds of balmy life in Hawaiʻi as lived on December 6, the day prior to the Pearl Harbor attack. The display of planes begins with an authentic Japanese Zero fighter set in a diorama portraying the deck of the Imperial Japanese Navy carrier *Hiryu* early in the morning of December 7. A U.S. Army Air Corps P-38 of the type that joined the fight that morning is on display, taking off from Haleʻiwa and Wheeler fields. The little-known story of the Battle of Niʻihau, the isolated "Forbidden island" off Kauaʻi, is told using the actual, very rare remains of a Japanese Zero, here the one that crash-landed on the Island following the attack. An actual B-25B Mitchell bomber, like the planes used in the famous 1942 Doolittle Raid on Japan, is on display; crewmen who flew in the raid have visited and left behind their signatures on the fuselage of the Mitchell bomber.

The tour moves on to the huge 80,000-square-foot seaplane Hangar 79, which still bears bullet holes from

the December 7 attack. Visitors get a look at ongoing restoration work on aircraft that will be displayed when ready, with craftsmen using actual World War II tools working on them. Here too is a display of restored aircraft used in the Korean War, including a MiG-15 and an F-86 Sabre.

Outside the hangars on the tarmac are planes from the Cold War and Vietnam War era placed on rotating display.

Visitors can take the controls of a P-38 chasing a Japanese Zero using computerized combat flight simulators loaded with a variety of air combat scenarios. A museum store offers classic World War II bomber nose art and model airplanes, aviation-themed Hawaiian shirts, books, and more. The Laniakea Café features gourmet hamburgers, sandwiches, salads, and daily specials.

The Pacific Aviation Museum Pearl Harbor is located on historic Ford Island, an active military base that is accessed by shuttle bus from the Pearl Harbor Visitor Center. Shuttles depart every fifteen minutes, from 9:00 a. m. to 4:00 p. m. daily. For security reasons, no bags are allowed on the shuttle bus to Ford Island. A bag storage facility, located at the *Bowfin* Submarine Park shuttle bus stop, stores belongings for a fee.

Those holding a military or DOD ID card can drive to the museum. Get on Ford Island Blvd. and drive over the Admiral Clarey Bridge. Enter the roundabout, turning 270 degrees to the left and take the third exit onto O'Kane Parkway. Drive south paralleling Luke Field Runway. Turn left onto Enterprise St. at the Red and White Control Tower. Then turn right into the Pacific Aviation Museum Pearl Harbor parking lot. ■

1

2

The collection at the Pacific Aviation Museum Pearl Harbor grows each year. Thanks to generous worldwide donations, curators have worked diligently to create a diverse and intriguing collection of aircraft. 1. From the impeccably restored Japanese Zero (Mitsubishi A6M2) housed in Hangar 37 to the up-and-coming restoration of a B-17 recovered from the swamps of New Guinea, there is a slice of aviation history for everyone. 2. Some of the planes and helicopters are found parked outside of Hanger 79, on the surrounding grounds, and some are housed inside the hangar. The displays are moved as needed to accommodate new arrivals and new restoration work. [Douglas Peebles]

OTHER MILITARY MUSEUMS

U.S. Army Museum of Hawai'i at Fort DeRussy, Waikīkī

The Hawai'i Army Museum is located on the grounds of the Hale Koa Hotel and the Ft. DeRussy Recreation Center in Waikīkī, inside the Battery Randolph Building. The displays at the museum tell the story of the military in Hawai'i from ancient times through the Vietnam War. Each era of military history is presented in separate displays featuring photographs and sound effects that create a "you were there" experience. The displays include ancient Hawaiian warfare, including Captain Cook and the Battle of Nu'uanu, Army Aviation, Winds of War (pre–Pearl Harbor attack Hawai'i), the attack of December 7, 1941, the 442nd Combat Regimental Team and the Americans of Japanese Ancestry in Hawai'i, and the Vietnam War. Vietnam-era tanks and a helicopter are among the artifacts displayed outside the museum.

The museum is open Tuesday through Saturday, 9 a.m.–5 p.m. Audio tours are available for rent. Admission is free; however, donations are welcome. Validated parking for the U.S. Army Museum of Hawai'i is at the Fort DeRussy parking facilities. With validation, the parking fee is discounted.

Tropic Lightning Museum at Schofield Barracks

The Tropic Lightning Museum at the U.S. Army base at Schofield Barracks displays the history of the base, the story of the Hawai'i-based Twenty-Fifth Infantry Division, and of nearby Wheeler Army Airfield, which was attacked along with Pearl Harbor on December 7, 1941.

Displays tell the history of the development of Schofield Barracks by the U.S. Army in the early 1900s and the harsh conditions overcome to construct the base. Curated exhibits tell the story of the Twenty-Fifth Infantry Division "Tropic Lightning" soldiers in combat during World War II, the Korean War, and the Vietnam War. On display outside the museum is a medium Sherman Tank with World War II markings, a Vulcan antiaircraft gun, and more.

Admission is free. The museum does not have a gift shop.

The Tropic Lightning Museum is located within Schofield Barracks on Wai'anae Ave., Bldg. 361, Scho-

field Barracks, HI 96875. It is open Tuesday–Saturday, 10:00 a.m.–4:00 p.m., and closed on federal holidays.

The public is invited to the on-post museum, but post visitors need to be issued a visitor's pass before entering. Access is through Lyman Gate off Kunia Road in Wahiawā in central O'ahu. Visitors must produce a photo ID at the Schofield Barracks gate for all adults, plus auto registration, insurance and safety check documents, or the rental car agreement for your vehicle. For additional information about visitor passes and up-to-date information about entering Schofield Barracks, go to www.garrison.hawaii.army.mil/des/default.htm.

Kāne'ohe Bay Pacific War Memorial

The Pacific War Memorial in Hawai'i is located at the entrance to Marine Corps Base-Hawai'i in Kāne'ohe.

The bronze statue is a copy of the National Iwo Jima Memorial that stands in Newington, Connecticut. The memorial depicts the iconic flag raising atop Mt. Suribachi on February 23, 1945, during the Battle of Iwo Jima, made famous by Joe Rosenthal's news photo. The Ko'olau Mountains and Kāne'ohe Bay provide a scenic backdrop. The statue was dedicated in 2002. The nonprofit Pacific War Memorial Association organized and raised the funds for the project. Plaques placed along the base of the statue tell the story of the U.S. Marine Corps divisions based in several Hawaiian Islands during World War II, including the Third Marine Division, the Fourth Marine Division, and the Fifth Marine Division, plus the Battle of Iwo Jima featuring the Mt. Suribachi flag raising.

Take the H-3 Freeway to the Windward Side end of the highway. For more information, see www.pacificwarmemorial.org.

Naval Air Museum Barbers Point

The Naval Air Museum at Barbers Point was opened to preserve aircraft that are related to the history of Naval Air Station Barbers Point and other aircraft linked to the history of naval aviation in Hawai'i. Plans call for restoring these aircraft and to educate the public. Visitors young and old can climb into the cockpit of a real fighter jet, don flight gear and have their picture taken. The museum collection includes four Navy fighter and attack jets, a Marine Corps Sea Stallion helicopter, and military ground vehicles. The nonprofit Naval Air Museum Barbers Point runs the museum. Admittance is by donation and only by making an appointment.

The museum is open by appointment only, Monday–Friday, 8:00 a.m.–4:30 p.m., and by appointment only Saturday–Sunday. Call (808) 682-3982 for more information or see www.nambarberspoint.org.

The museum's main office is located in Building 1792 on Midway Road at the former NAS Barbers Point airfield at the Kalaeloa Airport in southwest O'ahu. ■

1. **The U.S. Army Museum of Hawai'i is located at Fort DeRussy in Waikīkī. [U.S. Army]**

2. **The Tropic Lightning Museum is located in the heart of the historic district on Schofield Barracks. [U.S. Army]**

3. **Displays throughout the Tropic Lightning Museum reflect the history of Schofield Barracks, the 25th Infantry Division, and Wheeler Army Airfield. [U.S. Army]**

4. **Marines with 3rd Marine Regiment gather around the Pacific War Memorial, Marine Corps Base Hawai'i to conduct a safety brief before their regimental ride on October 10, 2013. [U.S. Marine Corps photo by Cpl. Matthew Callahan]**

MEDAL OF HONOR WINNERS

The Medal of Honor has been bestowed upon eighteen servicemen from Hawai'i. They fought in World War II, the Korean War, and the Vietnam War.

Twelve Americans of Japanese Ancestry men from Hawai'i who served in the 442nd Regimental Combat Team/100th Infantry Battalion received the Medal of Honor in 2000 in honor of their bravery in World War II battles.

Native Hawaiian winners of the Medal of Honor are Herbert Pilila'au from Wai'anae and Anthony Kaho'ohanohano from Kealakekua.

For bravery during the Pearl Harbor attack on December 7, 1941, fifteen men were awarded the Medal of Honor. They included the commander of the USS *Arizona,* Captain Franklin Van Valkenburgh of Minneapolis, who was killed directing operations from his exposed command deck.

In October 2012 more than fifty Medal of Honor recipients visited the National Memorial Cemetery of the Pacific at Punchbowl Crater. There they dedicated a special stone as a lasting tribute to Medal of Honor winners. As of 2012, thirty-two Medal of Honor winners were interred at the Punchbowl cemetery. ■

Medal of Honor Winners

	Branch	**Birth Place**	**Medal Accredited to:**
World War II			
Barney F. Hajiro	Army	Punēnē, Maui	Honolulu
Mikio Hasemoto	Army	Honolulu	Schofield Barracks
Shizuya Hayashi	Army	Waiakea	Schofield Barracks
Daniel K. Inouye	Army	Honolulu	Honolulu
Yeiki Kobashigawa	Army	Hilo	Honolulu
Robert Kuroda	Army	'Aiea	Honolulu
Kaoru Moto	Army	Spreckelsville, Maui	Spreckelsville, Maui
Masato Nakae	Army	Lihue, Kaua'i	Honolulu
Shinyei Nakamine	Army	Wai'anae	Honolulu
Allan M. Ohata	Army	Honolulu	Honolulu
Yukio Okutsu	Army	Koloa, Kaua'i	Koloa, Kaua'i
Francis B. Wai	Army	Honolulu	Honolulu
	Branch	**Birth Place**	**Medal Accredited to:**
Korean War			
Anthony T. Kaho'ohanohano	Army	Maui	Wailuku, Maui
Leroy A. Mendonca	Army	Honolulu	Honolulu
Herbert K Pilila'au	Army	Wai'anae	O'ahu
	Branch	**Birth Place**	**Medal Accredited to:**
Vietnam War			
Terry Teruo Kawamura	Army	Wahiawā	O'ahu
Elmelindo Rodriques Smith	Army	Honolulu	Honolulu
Rodney James Tadashi Yano	Army	Kealakekua	Honolulu
James Smith	Navy	Hawai'i	New York, NY
Humbert Roque Versace	Army	Honolulu	Norfolk, VA

HAWAIʻI AND THE KOREAN WAR

Hawaiʻi's people made a great sacrifice during the Korean War, losing more men per capita than any other U.S. state or territory. By the end of the war, 456 men from Hawaiʻi were killed or missing in action during the "Forgotten War." About 17,000 Hawaiʻi residents served as troops in the Korean War, yet unlike the veterans of World War I and World War II, there were no major victory parades when the war ended.

Three men from Hawaiʻi were awarded the Medal of Honor during the Korean War, which lasted from November 1950 until a cease-fire was called in July 1953.

In July 1953, U.S. Army Pfc. Herbert K. Pililaʻau of Waiʻanae was awarded the medal posthumously for heroic action on September 17, 1951. The Native Hawaiian was serving with Company C of the Twenty-Third Infantry Regiment when he was killed in action at the bloody battle at Heartbreak Ridge. Sgt. Leroy Mendonca of Honolulu, from Company B, Seventh Infantry Regiment, Third Infantry Division, was awarded the Medal of Honor posthumously for his selfless heroism near Chich-on on July 4, 1951. Anthony T. Kahoʻohanohano of Wailuku was posthumously awarded the Medal of Honor in 2011 at a White House ceremony. Kahoʻohanohano's Distinguished Service Cross for valor while serving with the Second Battalion, Seventeenth Infantry Regiment, Seventh Infantry Division near Chupari was upgraded to the Medal of Honor in response to a petition from his family.

The Schofield Barracks–based Tropic Lightning Division arrived in Korea early in the war, in July 1950, defending the port city of Pusan. Fourteen Tropic Lightning Division soldiers were awarded Medals of Honor, making the division one of the most decorated Army divisions of the Korean War.

The Thirty-Second Infantry Regiment, named "The Queen's Own" in 1916 by Queen Liliʻuokalani, engaged in a fighting withdrawal from the Chosin Reservoir in North Korean in late fall, 1950.

The Army's Twenty-Fourth Infantry Division was the first U.S. division to see action in the Korean War, given the mission of holding off the North Korean Army until more U.S. divisions could land in Korea. The Twenty-Fourth was first activated in Hawaiʻi in 1921 as the Hawaiian Division at Schofield Barracks. In recognition of its ties to Hawaiʻi, the Twenty-Fourth's insignia is a red taro leaf. The division was based at Schofield Barracks when Pearl Harbor was attacked and in 1942 shored up the coastal defenses of the North Shore of Oʻahu.

Hawaiʻi was most notably represented in the Korean War by the many local men who served in the Eighth Army's Fifth Regimental Combat Team Bobcats. In 1949, the Fifth was the last post–World War II occupation force to depart Korea, and then it was the first to return when war broke out between North and South Korea, with men from units organized at Schofield Barracks on Oʻahu providing a large part of the 178 officers and 3,129 enlisted men sent. They sailed away from Army Pier 40 at Honolulu Harbor and from Pearl Harbor aboard four troop ships. The Fifth carried on where the heroic Americans of Japanese Ancestry 442nd "Go for Broke" RCT left off at the end of World War II.

Once deployed in Korea, the Fifth saw combat for almost a year straight without significant breaks. In August 1950 the Fifth RCT was assigned to the Twenty-Fourth Infantry Division.

The fiftieth anniversary of end of the Korean War saw long-overdue honors being bestowed upon Hawaiʻi's Korean War veterans, raising interest and awareness of the Islands' contribution. Hawaiʻi's Korean War Memorial was dedicated in July 1994 on the State Capitol grounds. The six-foot-high, one-hundred-foot long, curving polished black granite wall honors both Korean War veterans and Vietnam War veterans from Hawaiʻi. One-foot-square markers on the wall name the 456 Hawaiʻi men who died in the Korean War. A month later, a charter was obtained for organization of a Korean War Veterans Association chapter for Hawaiʻi. Today there are chapters on Islands across the state. ■

HAWAI'I AND THE VIETNAM WAR

From the beginning of America's involvement in the Vietnam War, Hawai'i served as a training, supply, and air transportation base, as a rest and relaxation destination, and as the home of thousands of servicemen, both volunteers and those drafted, who saw action in Southeast Asia.

The first American combat troops posted to Vietnam were 100 helicopter gunners sent in 1963 from the Schofield Barracks–based Tropic Lightning Twenty-Fifth Infantry Division. The men were sent on temporary duty to serve with South Vietnam military units and flew aboard U.S. Army Bell H-21 Huey helicopters.

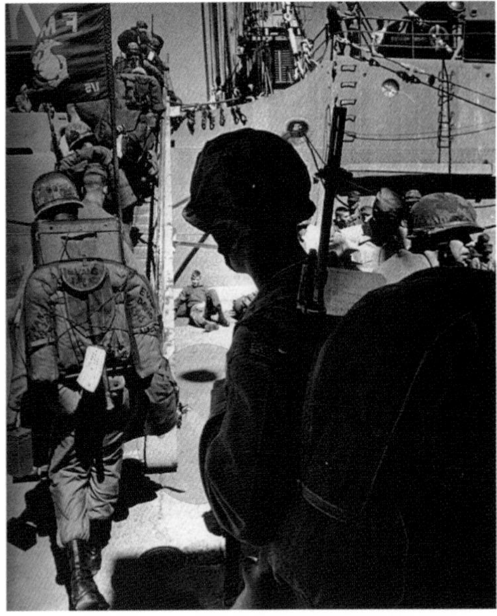

Hawai'i is the staging post for scores of thousands of Vietnam-bound troops. [*The Honolulu Advertiser*]

As a division, the Twenty-Fifth Infantry deployed from Schofield Barracks to Vietnam in 1966. In the year of the massive Tet Offensive, men from across the state were ordered to Schofield Barracks when the Hawai'i National Guard, Twenty-Ninth Infantry Brigade, was put on active duty. From this group, over 500 guardsmen fought in combat in Vietnam.

In the Marine Corps, all-Hawai'i Marine platoons were formed, with upwards of eighty local men going to Vietnam together to serve. Units of Marine fighter pilots deployed from Marine Corps Air Station Kāne'ohe Bay to Da Nang.

At Hickam Field, the U.S. Air Force provided military air transport services for servicemen and servicewomen and material flying to the war zone in Vietnam.

Tripler Army Medical Center provided care for the Vietnam wounded who required more than thirty days of in-hospital care.

Hickam Airfield hosted Operation Homecoming in 1973, when prisoner-of-war evacuees released from North Vietnam prisons were reunited with their families.

The Pearl Harbor Shipyard and Naval Station provided support for naval operations in Southeast Asia during the Vietnam War. Thousands of men returned from Vietnam aboard Navy ships sailing to Pearl Harbor.

In all, 276 men from Hawai'i were killed in the Vietnam War. Many were from rural O'ahu and Neighbor Island towns. Three local men serving in the U.S. Army were posthumously awarded the Medal of Honor: Corp. Terry Kawamura of Wahiawā, Platoon Sgt. Elmelindo Smith of Honolulu, and Air Calvary Sgt. Rodney Yano of Kealakekua on Hawai'i Island.

Fort DeRussy, the Hilton Hawaiian Village, and other Waikīkī hotels hosted servicemen on R&R. They were given a one-week pass after completing one year of service, with a set number of months spent out in the field—"in-country" in Vietnam-era lingo. Hawai'i was popular with family men who would meet their wives and sometimes also their children for a quick Waikīkī vacation. The R&R trip to Hawai'i took one day coming and one day going back to Vietnam, giving them a five-day stay in the Islands.

A memorial to Hawai'i's men and women who died while serving in the Vietnam War is located adjacent to the Hawai'i State Capitol. Each name has its own one-foot-square engraving on the curving, polished black granite wall.

A pavilion with a map detailing the Vietnam War was added to the World War II and Korean War pavilions at the National Memorial Cemetery of the Pacific. ■

1. Tom Kobashigawa of Kalihi, a POW since 1970, finally makes it home in 1973. [The Honolulu Advertiser]

2. Hawai'i goes to war in Vietnam: men of "Pineapple Company" in the field. [*The Honolulu Advertiser*]

3. Over the course of the Vietnam war, R&R flights bring close to a half-million servicemen back to Hawai'i. [*The Honolulu Advertiser*]

4. With child in arms, Luci Johnson Nugent, daughter of Lyndon B. Johnson, joins a throng of welcoming family and friends.

GULF WAR IRAQ-AFGHANISTAN

Kāne'ohe-based Marines take some time out to attend a memorial service at Kāne'ohe Marine Base Headquarters for ten Marines killed in Iraq, January 13, 2005. The honored dead include Lance Corporal Blake Magaoay from Pearl City. [*Honolulu Advertiser*/Craig T. Kojima]

onolulu ★ Star-Bulletin

AY, MARCH 20, 2003 / THE PULSE OF PARADISE / STARBULLETIN.COM / 50 CENTS ON OAHU •

R BEGINS

Chemical defense
Specialized mobile teams are in Kuwait, ready to detect and disarm weapons of mass destruction. **A2**

Lingle's advice
Gov. Linda Lingle asks those in the isles to remain calm, be vigilant and go about their lives. **A3**

Your opinion
Hawaii residents view the U.S. attack as everything from "justified" to "senseless." **A4**

Under siege
Bombing lights up the Iraqi capital, drawing anti-aircraft fire and setting Saddam's main complex ablaze. **A5**

NVASION

Coalition troops wear gas masks as Iraq fires missiles, but no chemicals detected

Air strikes rock Baghdad; Red Cross says initial attack kills at least 1, wounds 14

ASSOCIATED PRESS

Above, soldiers from the U.S. Army 3rd Battalion 15th Infantry aimed toward Iraq today while atop the last Kuwaiti berm before the border. Below, British Royal Air Force personnel waited in a bunker with their full nuclear, chemical and biological kits at a base in Kuwait after Iraqis fired missiles near them.

officials assure residents

Artillery fire signals start of ground war

promised: "The days of the Saddam Hussein regime are num-

Men and women stationed in Hawai'i and Hawai'i residents serving in the armed forces elsewhere took part in the Persian Gulf War's Operation Desert Storm in 1990–1991, as well as the conflicts launched following the post-9/11 terrorism attacks, including Operation Iraqi Freedom and Operation Enduring Freedom, the "War in Afghanistan." They represented the U.S. Army, the U.S. Navy, the Marine Corps, the U.S. Coast Guard, and the U.S. Air Force.

The USS *Missouri,* now home-ported at Pearl Harbor as a historical monument, provided firepower during Operation Desert Storm. The First Marine Expeditionary Brigade located at Marine Corps Air Station Kāne'ohe Bay was quickly deployed at the outbreak of the Persian Gulf War.

In 2003, the USS *Cheyenne,* a Pearl Harbor-based submarine, launched the first Tomahawk missile to begin the second Iraq War. The target was a bunker believed to be the location of Iraqi president Saddam Hussein.

In 2012, the Third Marine Regiment at Marine Corps Base Hawai'i celebrated their homecoming from Operation Enduring Freedom, rededicating their regimental battle colors, marking the end of the regiment's combat operations in Iraq and Afghanistan.

Also in 2012, the Twenty-Fifth Infantry Division's Third Brigade Combat Team (3,000 soldiers) was welcomed home from their yearlong mission with a parade at Schofield Barracks. Thousands of Hawai'i troops were then still stationed in Afghanistan, including 1,200 Kāne'ohe-based Marines and 2,000 soldiers from the Twenty-Fifth Combat Aviation Brigade.

Plans are underway for a memorial to these veterans to be built on O'ahu at a site yet to be determined. The memorial will honor those who served on air, land, or sea in one or more of the following: Persian Gulf War, Operation Desert Storm, Operation Iraqi Freedom, Operation Enduring Freedom, Operation New Dawn, the Global War on Terrorism, Homeland Defense, and Operation Noble Eagle. ■

1. **Marines of Marine Light Attack Helicopter Squadron 367 "Scarface" stand in formation during a welcome aboard ceremony at the Marine Corps Air Station, September 17, 2012. The squadron supported missions during Operations Desert Shield, Desert Storm, Iraqi Freedom and Enduring Freedom. [U.S. Marine Corps photo by Lance Cpl. James Sauter]**

2. **Soldiers with the Hawai'i Army National Guard's 29th Infantry Brigade Combat Team gather outside the headquarters of the 3rd Infantry Division and Regional Command (South) at Kandahar Airfield, Afghanistan, November12, 2012. Soldiers are, from left, Capt. Jonathan Joseph, Maj. Mark Mitsui, Sgt. Andrew Bowers, Chief Warrant Officer 2 Mel Masaki, Capt. Peter Ammerman, Capt. Brent Nakasone, Capt. Ralph Hasegawa, Capt. Eric Miyasato, Capt. Jake Kamihara, Lt. Col. Paul Takata and Capt. William Keahi. [U.S. Army photo by Staff Sgt. Brendan Mackie]**

3. **Marines and sailors of 3rd Marine Regiment are led by the unit's command element during a memorial run toward Boondocker training area, Marine Corps Base Hawai'i, for a ceremony commemorating the regiment's fallen Marines and sailors during Operations Iraqi Freedom and Enduring Freedom, June 1, 2012. [U.S. Marine Corps photo by Lance Cpl. James Sauter]**

A UH-1Y Huey aircraft with Marine Light Attack Helicopter Squadron 367, flies over Hawai'i, November 20, 2015. The unit gave Commandant of the Marine Corps, Gen. Robert B. Neller, and Sgt. Maj. of the Marine Corps Ronald L. Green, a tour of the O'ahu facilities during their Hawai'i visit. [U.S. Marine Corps photo by Staff Sgt. Gabriela Garcia/Released]

THE MILITARY
IN HAWAI'I
TODAY

Air Force

1. Senior Airman Mariah Akau with the 154th FSS is recognized as the Airman of the Year at 2015's Launa Ole awards which recognize the top individual and team performers for the past year. [U.S. Air National Guard photo by Senior Airman Orlando Corpuz]

2. A Hawai'i Air National Guard F-22 Raptor takes off from Joint Base Pearl Harbor-Hickam, September 26, 2015. [U.S. Air National Guard photo by Airman 1st Class Robert Cabuco]

3. Members of the Hickam Honor Guard perform as a firing party during the 74th attack on Hickam Field Remembrance Ceremony hosted by the 15th Wing on Joint Base Pearl Harbor-Hickam, December 7, 2015. Survivors and their family members attended the ceremony, which honors the men and women who lost their lives on Hickam Field during the two waves of attacks launched by the Imperial Japanese Navy on December 7, 1941. [U.S. Air Force photo by Tech. Sgt. Aaron Oelrich]

Army

1. Sgt. 1st Class Ryan Davison gives a block of instruction to a group of soldiers prior to a helocast into the water off the coast of Bellows Air Station, September 24, 2015. [U.S. Army photo by Staff Sgt. Armando R. Limon, 3rd Brigade Combat Team, 25th Infantry Division]

2. A Virginia Army National Guard soldier from Company B, 777th Aviation Support Battalion helps to establish a perimeter around a CH-47 Chinook during a downed aircraft recovery team exercise at Schofield Barracks, June 12, 2015. These soldiers are training to protect and recover aircraft effectively. [U.S. Army National Guard photo by Pfc. Paul D. Berzinas]

3. Soldiers assigned to 3rd Platoon, Company C, 2nd Battalion, 27th Infantry Regiment, 3rd Brigade Combat Team, 25th Infantry Division march in the Veterans Day parade at Wahiawā on November 11, 2015. [U.S. Army photo by Staff Sgt. Armando R. Limon, 3rd Brigade Combat Team, 25th Infantry Division]

4. From left: Governor of Hawai'i, David Y. Ige, Brig. Gen. Arthur J. Logan, Maj. Gen. Darryll D.M. Wong stand at attention during the adjutant general transfer of authority ceremony February 8, 2015 at Kalaeloa. Maj. Gen. Darryll D. M. Wong relinquished authority to Brig. Gen. Arthur J. Logan as the new adjutant general. [U.S. Army photo by Staff Sgt. Ryan Sheldon, 117th Mobile Public Affairs Detachment]

Navy

1. Mayor Kirk Caldwell (left) and Navy Capt. Mark S. Manfredi observe the ceremony at Honolulu Hale during the 10th annual Mayor's Remembrance Walk, September 6, 2015. Dignitaries, various government agencies, first responders, organizations and other members of the community honored lives lost in the Sept. 11, 2001, attacks with a walk through Honolulu. [U.S. Marine Corps photo by Kristen Wong]

2. General Lori J. Robinson, commander Pacific Air Forces (left) and Honorable Judge Thomas Kaulukukui Jr. lay a wreath during the 66th Mayor's Memorial Day Ceremony at the National Memorial Cemetery of the Pacific at Punchbowl, May 25, 2015. [U.S. Navy photo by Mass Communication Specialist 2nd Class Laurie Dexter]

3. Lt. Erik Guiremand, assigned to the guided-missile destroyer USS *Paul Hamilton* (DDG 60), passes through sideboys as he detaches from the command prior to the ship's departure from Joint Base Pearl Harbor-Hickam for a scheduled independent deployment to the Arabian Gulf and Western Pacific Ocean, February 14, 2015. [U.S. Navy photo by Mass Communication Specialist 2nd Class Diana Quinlan]

1, 2. **Navy chief petty officers and chief petty officer selects stand at parade rest during a Pearl Harbor honors and heritage "morning colors" ceremony at the World War II Valor in the Pacific National Monument Visitor Center on Joint Base Pearl Harbor-Hickam, August 20, 2015. Hosted by Navy Region Hawai'i in coordination with the National Park Service, the theme for the ceremony was the 70th anniversary of the end of the war in the Pacific in honor of those who have served and are currently serving the nation. The event also recognized approximately 40 Navy chief petty officer selects in attendance. [U.S. Navy photo by Mass Communication Specialist 2nd Class Johans Chavarro]**

3. **Firecontrolman 1st Class Michael Farbridge-Currie, assigned to the guided-missile destroyer USS *Paul Hamilton*, kisses his daughter as the ship prepares for departure from Joint Base Pearl Harbor-Hickam for a scheduled independent deployment to the Arabian Gulf and Western Pacific Ocean, February 14, 2015. [U.S. Navy photo by Mass Communication Specialist 2nd Class Diana Quinlan]**

1. U.S. Navy Landing Craft Air Cushion conduct amphibious assault operations during the MARFORPAC-hosted U.S. Pacific Command Amphibious Leaders Symposium at Bellows, May 19, 2015. [U.S. Marine Corps photo by Lance Cpl. Aaron S. Patterson]

2. U.S. Navy Sailors hold lei to give to specials guests attending a Change of Command Ceremony aboard Marine Corps Air Station, Kāne'ohe Bay, January 16, 2015. [U.S. Marine Corps photo by Lance Cpl. Julian Temblador, MCBH Combat Camera]

3. More than 300 chief petty officers and first class petty officers across Hawai'i gather for a lesson in Naval heritage atop Makapu'u Point trail. [U.S. Navy photo by Mass communication Specialist 1st Class Brian McNeal]

Marines

1. Marine scout snipers with Weapons Company, 2nd Battalion, 3rd Marine Regiment, conduct high angle shooting on Range 10 aboard Marine Corps Base Hawai'i, April 8, 2015. [U.S. Marine Corps photo by Sgt. Sarah Dietz]

2. Members of 1st Battalion, 3rd Marine Regiment dredge through the mud in Nu'upia Ponds to haul out a log polluting the area during a cleanup held June 8, 2015. [U.S. Marine Corps photo by Christine Cabalo]

3. The U.S. Marine Corps Forces, Pacific color guard presents arms during the relief and appointment ceremony on Camp H. M. Smith, July 23, 2015. [U.S. Marine Corps photo by Lance Cpl. Maximiliano Rosas]

1. A CH-53E Super Stallion helicopter flies above Marine Corps Training Area Bellows after completing a portion of a simulated joint Downed Aircraft Recovery Team exercise, July 30, 2015. The exercise was comprised of service members from all branches of the United States military. [U.S. Marine Corps photo by Cpl. Brittney Vito]

2. A cast master with 3rd Squadron, 4th Cavalry Regiment, 3rd Brigade Combat Team out of Schofield Barracks, also known as "Comanche Troop," signals to the jumpers to move forward and enter the water during helocast operations at Marine Corps Training Area Bellows, Sept. 23, 2015. The unit was refining their waterborne insertion tactics and re-qualifying their cast masters for future deployments and reconnaissance missions. For most helocast insertions, the aircraft assumes an altitude just above the water's surface, with airspeed of 10 knots or less. Team members then exit the aircraft and enter the water. [U.S. Marine Corps photo by Cpl. Brittney Vito]

3. Sgt. Joshua Flores, the training noncommissioned officer of Combat Logistics Battalion 3, crawls his way through the crashing surf at Fort Hase beach aboard Marine Corps Base Hawai'i during a training scenario in Sergeants Course Aug. 19, 2015. Sergeants Course is a vital part of professional military education for any Marine and helps to maintain the standards amongst the NCOs of the Marine Corps. [U.S. Marine Corps photo by Cpl. Khalil Ross]

1. **Marines and Sailors with Company A, 1st Reconnaissance Battalion, 1st Marine Division, pose for a photo atop of the USS *Mississippi,* aboard Joint Base Pearl Harbor-Hickam, November 17, 2015. [U.S. Marine Corps photo by Sgt. Tony Simmons]**

2. **President Barack Obama and first lady Michelle Obama speak to service members at Anderson Hall aboard Marine Corps Base Hawai'i, December 25, 2015. [U.S. Marine Corps photo by Cpl. Adam Koroley]**

3. **Col. Sean C. Killeen and Sgt. Maj. Gregory L. Hall pose for a photo with members of the Kāne'ohe Bay Air Show promotion crew during the 69th Annual Kailua Independence Day Parade, July 4, 2015. [U.S. Marine Corps photo by Lance Cpl. Harley Thomas]**

TIMELINE OF MILITARY HISTORY IN HAWAI'I

1778—Captain James Cook of the Royal British Navy lands at Waimea, Kaua'i, introduces gunpowder, musket, pistol, steel hand weapons, cannon to Hawai'i.

1779—Captain Cook is killed by Hawaiian warriors during a skirmish with British marines at Kealakekua Bay.

1782—King Kamehameha given control of Hawaiian god of war, Kūkā'ilimoku.

1790—Kamehameha continues consolidation of the Island of Hawai'i from his base in North Kohala, fighting against Puna. After battle at Ka'ū, warriors under Keōua are killed by poisonous gas from Kīlauea Volcano.

1791—Pu'ukoholā Heiau at Kawaihae completed to fulfill prophecy of Kamehameha controlling all Islands through military conquest.

1792—British sailors living in Hawai'i, Isaac Davis and John Young, advise Kamehameha on Western arms and tactics and train his troops in the use of firearms.

1795—Kamehameha's armada of 960 war canoes and 10,000 soldiers captures Maui and Moloka'i at the Battle of Kawela. Army moves on to O'ahu to fight the Battle of Nu'uanu. Troops land at Wai'alae and Waikīkī beaches, fighting near Punchbowl and up to the edge of Nu'uanu Pali, where hundreds of opposing warriors are forced over the pali to their deaths.

1796—Kamehameha decimates Ka'ū rebel forces under Namakea at Battle of Kaipalaoa at Hilo in his last major battle.

1796—Peleleu canoe troop carrying fleet from Wai'anae hits storm crossing Kaua'i Channel, halting planned invasion of Kaua'i.

1803—Kamehameha again organizes invasion force to take Kaua'i, but epidemic devastates troops; invasion is called off.

1815—Attempt by Russian American Company to build a blockhouse fort at Honolulu Harbor fails. Kamehameha builds large coral block fort on site.

1819—Following death of Kamehameha and fall of kapu system, pro-kapu army rallied by Kekuaokalani is vanquished at Battle of Kuamo'o, a coastal lava field south of Keauhou on Hawai'i Island.

1824—Battle of Wahiawā pits rebel Kaua'i forces against superior army of koa soldiers transported from O'ahu and other windward Islands under Kamehameha's general Kalanimoku. Kaua'i rebels slaughtered on plains of Wahiawā, and Kamehameha dynasty consolidates control of Kaua'i.

1843—British Navy captain Lord George Paulet seizes lightly defended Honolulu with one man-of-war ship, creates British-run military force made up of Hawaiian soldiers. Is later removed by British commander of the Pacific and sovereignty returned to Kamehameha III.

1861–1865—Kingdom of Hawai'i remains neutral during Civil War. Sons of missionaries and Native Hawaiians fight in war enrolled as Sandwich islanders. Punahou graduate Samuel Chapman Armstrong becomes general, leads black Union soldiers.

1873—One hundred and fifty armed U.S. Marines land at request of Kingdom of Hawai'i to help quell election riot over loss by Queen Emma to King Kalākaua.

1885—Pro-annexation Honolulu Rifles militia is formed. Kalākaua signs Reciprocity Treaty granting U.S. War Department use of Pearl Harbor as coaling station.

1889—Native Hawaiian Robert Wilcox returns from artillery training in Italy and attempts overthrow of monarchy in wake of signing of "Bayonet Constitution." Eight of his men are killed in failed attempt.

1893—In January Marines land from USS *Boston,* take post near Queen Lili'uokalani's home as her Kingdom of Hawai'i is overthrown by pro-American annexation Committee of Safety.

1895—Troops of Republic of Hawai'i, formed in 1894, battle Native Hawaiian fugitive leper Kaluaiko'olau at Battle of Kalalau on Kaua'i.

1898, August 12—The United States ratifies the treaty of annexation of Hawai'i.

1900—Hawaiian Islands become Territory of Hawai'i under U.S. control. Territorial status opens door to later federal funding of port improvements across Hawai'i to allow for rapid deployment of troops in case of invasion.

1903—U.S. warships carrying 3,000 men arrive in Honolulu Harbor to take on supplies. The warships include the cruisers *New Orleans, Albany, Cincinnati,* and *Raleigh;* battleships *Wisconsin* and *Oregon;* and the flagship *Kentucky.*

1915, March 25—The U.S. Navy submarine *Skate* (F-4), one of four based in the Islands, explodes and sinks 306 feet to the bottom about three-quarters of a mile off Honolulu Harbor, killing the twenty-one-man crew. The incident is the first submarine disaster in American naval history.

1916, February 4—The crews of seven interned steamships, including the German cruiser *Geier,* set their vessels on fire to prevent them from being used by the U.S. military. The United States is officially neutral in the conflict until declaring war with Germany on April 6, 1917.

1923—The Pearl Harbor barracks become the home of the U.S. Marine Corps.

1927—The War Memorial Natatorium is built on the waterfront at the eastern end of Waikīkī as a memorial to the 179 men and women of the Hawaiian Islands that died as soldiers in World War I.

1941, December 7—Japanese bombers attack Pearl Harbor, entering the United States into World War II.

1942, June 4—American fighter pilots and dive bombers sink four carriers of the Japanese naval fleet near Midway Atoll in the Battle of Midway, securing the strategic Navy base location for the duration of the war.

1942, June 5—Admiral Nimitz (1885–1966), the commander of the Pacific Fleet, announces the victory over the Japanese Fleet at Midway. The Battle of Midway becomes a turning point in World War II.

1943, February 1—The government announces the formation of the all-Nisei (second-generation Japanese American) 442nd Infantry Regimental Combat Team. About 10,000 Hawai'i Nisei volunteer within days, though only 1,256 mainland Nisei volunteer. The volunteers want to demonstrate their loyalty to the United States despite the harsh racism they experience in the wake of the Pearl Harbor attack.

1943, September 2—The all-Nisei 100th Infantry Battalion from Hawai'i lands in Oran, North Africa, then in June of 1944 they are joined by the 442nd Infantry Regiment.

1944, February 13—The U.S. Navy submarine rescue vehicle USS *Macaw,* on a mission to retrieve the submarine USS *Flier,* runs aground at Midway Atoll due to bad weather. A crew mans the ship's pumps until a March storm finishes off the vessel.

1944–1946—Five thousand Italian prisoners of war captured in 1943 by the British in North Africa are held at four locations on O'ahu: Schofield, Kalihi Valley, Kāne'ohe, and Sand Island.

1945, June—About 250,000 Army troops and 250,000 Navy and Marine Corps members are stationed in the Hawaiian Islands. Millions of servicemen pass through the Islands on their way to combat areas in the Pacific.

1945, August 15—Victory over Japan Day ("V-J Day") is declared after the United States drops nuclear bombs on Japan in Hiroshima (August 6) and Nagasaki (August 9).

1945, September 2—The forces of Japan officially surrender on the deck of the USS *Missouri* battleship.

1948—Sixteen of twenty crew members of a fully loaded B-29 Superfortress are killed in a fiery crash at Hickam field.

1950, June 25—North Korea invades South Korea, beginning the Korean War. The United States sends troops to the war, including an estimated 17,000 Hawaiian residents; 341 are killed with another 79 missing in action. The war ends on July 27, 1953.

1950—From November 27 to December 9, the U.S. First Marine Division, including the Thirty-Second Infantry Regiment named "The Queen's Own" by Queen Lili'uokalani in 1916, engage in a fighting withdrawal from the Chosin Reservoir in North Korea. Facing extremely low temperatures as well as huge numbers of Chinese troops, the U.S. forces inflict heavy damage on ten Chinese infantry divisions.

1957—Four Air Force members are killed when their six-jet B-47 bomber crashes into a Wai'anae Range mountainside at 400 miles per hour.

1958—The communist regime of North Vietnam invades South Vietnam, beginning the Vietnam War. The conflict lasts until 1975, with 221 Hawaiian residents dying in the war and an estimated 13,000 Hawaiian residents taking part, including many who are wounded and then treated at O'ahu's Tripler Army Medical Center.

1959—The *Swordfish* becomes the first nuclear submarine to homeport in Pearl Harbor.

1963–1971—The Schofield Barracks–based U.S. Army Twenty-Fifth Infantry Division (nicknamed "Tropic Lightning") fights in the Vietnam War beginning in 1963, when 100 helicopter door gunners are deployed. The Twenty-Fifth fights in some of the toughest battles of the war, including Operation Junction City. During the Tet Offensive, the division defends Saigon. Twenty-two Medals of Honor are awarded to Tropic Lightning soldiers during the Vietnam War.

1990–1991—First Gulf War in the Persian Gulf in response to Iraq's invasion of Kuwait. The war eventually requires the services of more than 7,000 troops based in Kāne'ohe before Iraq accepts United Nations conditions and resolutions.

1993—Kaua'i's Pacific Missile Range Facility begins conducting STARS missile tests.

1994—The Korean-Vietnam War Memorial is dedicated at Hawai'i's State Capitol in Honolulu.

2004, July—The biennial Rim of the Pacific (RIMPAC) naval exercises take place in Hawaiian waters from June 29 to July 27 and involve more than thirty-five ships, ninety aircraft, seven submarines, and 11,000 soldiers, airmen, sailors, Marines, and Coast Guardsmen.

2016, January 14—Twelve Marines from the 1st Marine Aircraft Wing at Marine Corps Base Hawai'i were lost at sea when two CH-53E helicopters went down off the North Shore of O'ahu during a nighttime training mission flight.

Chronology of Military Bases in Hawai'i

1887—King Kalākaua signs a lease granting use of Pearl Harbor by the United States for eight years as a result of the Reciprocity Treaty.

1898, August 16—Camp McKinley, a tent encampment of U.S. infantry and engineers, is set up at Waikīkī's Kapi'olani Park. This is the first U.S. Army camp in the Islands and home to the First New York Volunteer Infantry Regiment.

1905—Kahauiki Military Reservation is established in Honolulu, becoming Hawai'i's first permanent U.S. Army post. The post is renamed Shafter Military Reservation in 1907 in honor of Civil War Medal of Honor winner, Major General William R. Shafter (1835–1906).

1906—Fort Ruger Military Reservation is established at Diamond Head (Lē'ahi). The reservation is named in honor of Major General Thomas H. Ruger, who served from 1871 to 1876 as the superintendent of the U.S. Military Academy at West Point. A network of tunnels is carved into the mountain, and cannon emplacements are placed atop the crater rim along with observation posts and bunkers. The fort includes Battery Harlow (1910–1943); Battery Birkhimer (1916–1943); Battery Granger Adams (1935–1946); Battery Dodge (1915–1925); Battery Mills (1916–1925); Battery 407 (1944); Bat-

tery Hulings (1915–1925); and Battery Ruger (1937–1943).

1907—Fort Armstrong is built on Honolulu's Ka'ākaukukui Reef near Kalehuawehe, a place known for its healing, cleansing baths. Fort Armstrong is named after Brigadier General Samuel C. Armstrong (1839–1893), son of a missionary, the Rev. Richard Armstrong (1805–1860) who arrived in 1832.

1907—Fort Kamehameha Military Reservation is established at the entrance to Pearl Harbor, becoming the only U.S. fort to be named after a foreign king. Soon constructed is a series of coastal artillery batteries, a "Ring of Steel" including long-range guns and mortars to fortify O'ahu's harbors. Coastal batteries at Fort Kamehameha included the following: Battery Selfridge (1911), the first to be constructed at Fort Kamehameha, with two twelve-inch disappearing rifles able to fire 1,046-pound projectiles 17,000 yards; Battery Randolph (1911); Battery Jackson (1914), with two six-inch guns able to fire 106-pound projectiles 14,600 yards; Battery Hawkins (1914), with two three-inch rapid-fire rifled cannon able to fire fifteen-pound projectiles 11,100 yards (within range of the entrance to Pearl Harbor); Battery Hasbrouck (1914), with eight twelve-inch mortars able to fire projectiles 15,200 yards; and Battery Closson (1920), with two twelve-inch guns able to fire 975-pound projectiles 17.1 miles.

1908—Construction of naval facilities begin in Pearl Harbor, formerly known by the Hawaiian name Pu'uloa.

1909—Schofield Barracks Military Reservation is established on 14,000 acres in Wahiawā, O'ahu, eventually becoming the biggest permanent U.S. Army post. The base is named for President Andrew Johnson's secretary of war, Lieutenant General John M. Schofield (1831–1906).

1915—Fort DeRussy is constructed to protect Pearl Harbor and Honolulu. Two battery locations within the fort hold large cannons, which are later replaced with antiaircraft guns. The fort is disbanded on June 28, 1950. The guns were removed and the site was designated an Armed Forces Recreation Area. In the 1970s the fort's Battery Randolph became home to the U.S. Army Museum of Hawai'i.

1917—Camp McCarthy opens on the grounds of the old state capitol as a State National Guard camp.

1917—Pearl Harbor (Ford Island) Military Reservation (Pearl Harbor Naval Base) is designed to protect Pearl Harbor, and the site includes Battery Adair (1917–1925) and Battery Boyd (1917–1925).

1918—Pearl Harbor naval station is established.

1919—An Army-Navy air facility opens at Luke Field on Ford Island.

1921—Barbers Point Military Reservation is established at Barbers Point Beach. Battery Barbers Point is operational from 1937 to 1942.

1922—Wheeler Field, now known as Wheeler Air Force Base, is established in Wahiawā, O'ahu, near Schofield Barracks. The base is named after Sheldon H. Wheeler, an Air Force major who died in a plane crash in 1921.

1939—Kāne'ohe Bay is dredged by the Navy to create an air station, but the unit stationed there is decommissioned in 1949 and moved to Barbers Point Naval Air Station. The Kāne'ohe Bay location is reopened in 1952 as Marine Corps Air Station Kane'ohe Bay.

1949, September 2—The National Memorial Cemetery of the Pacific (known locally as Punchbowl) is dedicated to men and women who served in the armed forces. To date about 53,000 veterans and their dependents have been interred in the cemetery, which is located in the extinct volcanic crater called Punchbowl.

1993—A federal commission votes to close the Barbers Point site, also known by its Hawaiian name Kalaeloa, which is returned to the State in 1999.

BIBLIOGRAPHY

Ainsworth, Gail, and Bren Bailey. *Maui Remembers: A Local History.* Honolulu: Mutual Publishing, 1994.

Brown, DeSoto, and Anne Ellett. *Hawaii Goes to War: Life in Hawaii from Pearl Harbor to Peace.* Honolulu: Editions Ltd., 1989.

Clark, Blake. *Remember Pearl Harbor!* New York: Modern age Books, 1942.

Cook, Chris. *A Kaua'i Reader.* Honolulu, Hawaii: Mutual Publishing, 1995.

Cook, Chris, and Boynton, David. *New Kauai Movie Book Films Made on the Garden Island.* Mutual Publishing, 2013.

Daws, Gavan. Honolulu: *The First Century.* Honolulu: Mutual Publishing, 2006.

Desha, Stephen, and Frances N. Frazier. *Kamehameha and His Warrior Kekūhaupi'o.* Honolulu: Kamehameha Schools Press, 2000.

Dukas, Neil Bernard. *A Military History of Sovereign Hawai'i.* Honolulu, Hawaii: Mutual Publishing, 2004.

Dukas, Neil Bernard. *The Battle of Nu'uanu, 1795: An Illustrated Pocket Guide to the O'ahu Battlefield.* Honolulu, Hawai'i: Mutual Publishing, 2010.

Feher, Joseph, Edward Joesting, and O. A. Bushnell. *Hawaii; A Pictorial History.* Honolulu: Bishop Museum Press, 1969.

Grant, Glen, and Bennett Hymer. *Hawai'i Looking Back: An Illustrated History of the Islands.* Honolulu, Hawai'i: Mutual Publishing, 2000.

Jones, Syd. *Before and Beyond the Niihau Zero: The Unlikely Drama of Hawaii's Forbidden Island Prior to, During, and After the Pearl Harbor Attack.* CreateSpace Independent Publishing Platform, 2014.

Judd, Walter F. *Hawaii Joins the World.* Honolulu: Mutual Publishing, 1998.

Kamakau, Samuel Manaiakalani, and Samuel Manaiakalani Kamakau. *Ruling Chiefs of Hawaii.* Honolulu: Kamehameha Schools Press, 1992.

Mesick, Lilian Shrewsbury, and Wallace Rider Farrington. *The Kingdom of Hawaii.* Honolulu: Printed by Porter Print. Co., 1934.

Paradise of the Pacific. December 1936 Holiday Issue. Honolulu, Hawaiian Islands: Press Pub. Co.

Rampell, Ed, and Reyes, Luis I. *Hawaii Movie and Television Book Celebrating 100 Years of Film Production Throughout the Hawaiian Islands.* Mutual Publishing, 2013.

Rampell, Ed, and Luis Reyes. *Pearl Harbor in the Movies.* Honolulu, HI: Mutual Publishing, 2001.

Schweitzer, Sophia V. *Big Island Journey: An Illustrated Narrative of the Island of Hawai'i.* Honolulu, Hawai'i: Mutual Publishing, 2009.

Seiden, Allan. *Pearl Harbor: From Fishponds to Warships: A Complete Illustrated History.* Honolulu: Mutual Publishing, 2001.

Sunshine, Linda, Antonia Felix, Jerry Bruckheimer, and Michael Bay. *Pearl Harbor: The Movie and the Moment.* New York: Hyperion, 2001.

Wright, Theon. *Rape in Paradise.* Honolulu: Mutual Publishing, 2005.

Young, Lucien. *The Boston at Hawaii; or, The observations and Impressions of a Naval Oficer During a Stay of Fourteen Months in Those Islands on a Man-of-War.* Washington, D.C.: Gibson Bros., 1898.

Websites and Films

Ford Island History–Hawaii Aviation An Archive of Historic Photos and Facts–hawaii.gov/hawaiiaviation/hawaii-airfields-airports/oahu-pre-world-war-ii/ford-island

From Here to Eternity–Adler, Buddy, Fred Zinnemann, Daniel Taradash, Burt Lancaster, Frank Sinatra, Montgomery Clift, Donna Reed, Deborah Kerr, and James Jones. Burbank: Columbia Tristar Home Video, 1994.

Hawai'i Medal of Honor Winners–www.homeofheroes.com/moh/states/hi.html

Library of Congress–Chronicling America–Historic American Newspaper–chroniclingamerica.loc.gov/

National Memorial Cemetery of the Pacific–www.cem.va.gov/cems/nchp/nmcp.asp

National Park Service–World War II Valor in the Pacific www.nps.gov/valr/index.htm

442nd Regimental Combat Team–Go For Broke National Educational Center - www.goforbroke.org/history/history_historical_veterans_442nd.asp

100th Infantry Battalion Veterans–Education Center, Varsity Victory Volunteers–www.100thbattalion.org/history/japanese-american-units/varsity-victory-volunteers/

History of Forts in Hawai'i–U.S. Army Pacific–www.usarpac.army.mil/history.asp

Pacific Aviation Museum Pearl Harbor–www.pacificaviationmuseum.org

Public Broadcasting System–History Detectives Special Investigations–The Ni'ihau Incident–www.pbs.org/opb/historydetectives/investigation/the-niihau-incident/

The Hawaiians–Gries, Tom, Walter Mirisch, Charlton Heston, Geraldine Chaplin, John Phillip Law, and James A. Michener. Los Angeles: Metro-Goldwyn-Mayer Studios Inc., 2010.

Tora! Tora! Tora!–Fleischer, Richard, Elmo Williams, Toshio Masuda, Kinji Fukasuka, Larry Forrester, Hideo Oguni, Ryūzō Kikushima, et al. Beverly Hills: Twentieth Century Fox Home Entertainment., 2001.

Tropic Lightning Museum–www.garrison.hawaii.army.mil/tlm/index.html

USS *Bowfin* Museum–www.bowfing.org

USS *Missouri*–www.ussmissouri.com

Waikiki Natatorium War Memorial–www.natatorium.org/

INDEX

I

J

K

V

W

Y

ABOUT THE AUTHORS

Hawai'i-based Chris Cook is editor of A Guide to Pearl Harbor and Ford Island Historic Military Sites as well as other books on Hawai'i's past. A graduate of the University of Hawai'i at Manoa, he is the former editor of The Garden Island newspaper. His articles on the history of World War II on Kaua'i appeared frequently during the war's fiftieth anniversary years 1991-1995. Prior to his career in journalism, Cook was employed by a World War II Navy SeaBee veteran and post-war military contractor and worked on jobs at Pearl Harbor, Schofield Barracks, Kaneohe Marine Corps Air Station and other military bases across the Hawaiian Islands plus remote Johnston (Kalama) Atoll.

Lieutenant General Emerson "Emo" Gardner, USMC (ret.) completed 37 years of distinguished service as a Marine officer in 2010 and now has a strategic consulting practice in Arlington, VA. From 2002 to 2004, he was the Director for Operations at US Pacific Command at Camp Smith, Hawaii where he coordinated US joint military and interagency operations in the Pacific theater. He lives both in Honolulu and Arlington, VA.

Photo Credits

The following photos are from dreamstime.com:

background flag, pages i, 82, 128-142: © Michael Flippo
trunk, pages i, iii: © Danaichidsin
image under caption, pages ii, 20, 109: © Andrey Kuzmin
star, page v: © Sivitri
banner with stars, pages vi, viii, ix, 2, 8, 11, 16, 18, 23, 26, 30, 31, 44, 52, 56, 61, 66, 70, 73, 82, 84, 90, 92, 97, 99, 104, 107, 108, 110, 112, 113, 114, 116, 128, 132, 134, 141, 142: © Ryan Jorgensen
plane, pages vi, 33: © Kojihirano
background, pages vi-vii: © Rolfgeorg Brenner
bag, page vii: © Exopixel
background, page viii: © Kashamalasha
background, pages ix, 30, 95, 103, 112: © Kashamalasha
submarine porthole, pages x, 14, 28, 30, 42: © Andreykuzmin
background, pages 2-13: © Phatthanit Roengsamran
background in sidebars, pages 3, 39, 69, 74, 76, 78, 93: © Alexei Novikov
background, pages 20-21: © Kashamalasha
photo frames, page 21: © Andreykuzmin
sunburst, pages 32, 35: © Luceluceluce
gas mask, page 45: © Briancweed
tire, page 46: © Dule964
bond, page 50: © Rosemary Buffoni
background, pages 52-555: © Magdav997
background, pages 70-72: © Hypermania37
plane, page 72: © Plutonius
camera, page 5: © Konstantin32
postcard, page 76: © Mcarrel
postcard, page 77: © Konstantin32
background, pages 78-79: © Tamara Kulikova
photo corners, page 79: © Lou Oates
negative frame, page 79: © Grungemaster
background, pages 80-81: © Wandall
sailor hat, page 82: © Peanutroaster
film strip, pages 84-87: © Flas100
crossroads sign, page 98: © Ldionisio
background, page 106: © Chris Curtis
plane, page 109: © Alex Sudaricov
Korean flag, page 13: © Vera08
airforce star, page 120: © Robin2b
wreath, page 122: © Sphraner
Marine flag, page 125: © Americanspirit